THE
ENCHANTMENT
OF
NEW YORK

75 OF MANHATTAN'S MOST MAGICAL AND UNIQUE ATTRACTIONS

Willem Post and Ton Wienbelt
TRANSLATED BY JASMINE VAN DEN HOEK
JASMINE JADE WRITING AND EDITING

T0040243

Skyhorse Publishing

Skyhorse Publishing books may be purchased in bulk at special discounts for sales promotion, corporate gifts, fund-raising, or educational purposes. Special editions can also be created to specifications. For details, contact the Special Sales Department, Skyhorse Publishing, 307 West 36th Street, 11th Floor, New York, NY 10018 or info@skyhorsepublishing.com.

Skyhorse® and Skyhorse Publishing® are registered trademarks of Skyhorse Publishing, Inc.®, a Delaware corporation.

Visit our website at www.skyhorsepublishing.com.

10 9 8 7 6 5 4 3 2 1

Library of Congress Cataloging-in-Publication Data

Names: Post, Willem, 1955- author. | Wienbelt, Ton, photographer.
Title: The enchantment of New York: 75 of Manhattan's most magical and
   unique attractions / Willem Post and Ton Wienbelt.
Other titles: Magie van New York. English
Description: New York : Skyhorse Publishing, 2016.
Identifiers: LCCN 2016009369| ISBN 9781510708112 (pbk.: alk. paper) | ISBN
   9781510708129 (ebook)
Subjects: LCSH: Manhattan (New York, N.Y.)—Guidebooks. | Manhattan (New
   York, N.Y.)—Description and travel. | New York (N.Y.)—Guidebooks. | New
   York (N.Y.)—Description and travel.
Classification: LCC F128.18 .P6813 2016 | DDC 917.47/104—dc23 LC record available
at http://lccn.loc.gov/2016009369

Cover design by Jane Sheppard
Cover photographs by Ton Wienbelt

Print ISBN: 978-1-5107-0811-2
Ebook ISBN: 978-1-5107-0812-9

Printed in China

Contents

Many travel books have already been written about New York. They are often filled with so many dizzying facts that lead a credulous visitor away from the true New York. This book is different. *The Enchantment of New York* offers a handy and manageable choice of seventy-five remarkable places that reflect the diversity of the city. This selection is based on our own preferences, with some parts recommended by other New York adepts.

Being able to make this book has been an absolute pleasure. I met Ton Wienbelt when I was writing my American election magazine at the start of 2012 in his design studio in The Hague. From his cupboard of hundreds of books he helped design, I picked up an American photo book of New York. It was as if I pressed a button. "New York is the most photogenic city in the world. Breathtaking. My dream is to, one day, make a book about New York myself," said my new friend. It turned out that Ton had already taken thousands of photos of the Big Apple in previous years. They were all neatly stored on his computer. What strikes me about Ton's photos is the meticulous search for

reality—from the way in which the light falls upon the city, to the faces of people as they really are. Ton has an eye for detail for what can be exposed as art in the city: the small yet remarkable parts of street life, but also a building or artwork in a broad architectural context. We quickly sealed the deal. He shoots, I write. We traveled to New York several times together. Ton resided there in the autumn of 2013. To begin our zigzag tour through Manhattan, we met in the Lower East Side, one of the most fascinating neighborhoods. Soon we came to realize the city we claimed to know like the back of our hands had many surprises in store for us. We had a lot of catching up to do for this book.

Many of the most famous hot spots you will be able to find for yourself. When you're in New York for the first time, of course you will go up the Empire State Building, travel by free ferry to Staten Island to see the Statue of Liberty ("the Dutch excursion"), and take an evening stroll through Times Square in a sea of light amid the bustling people. Our first piece of advice: if you're there anyway, you might as well visit the rotating restaurant, The View, above the Marriott Marquis hotel and enjoy the magical dancing lights from the skyscrapers in the dark distance. In this book we want to show you the places we found most remarkable, from the reasonably well known to the completely unknown. But—hopefully—always surprising. As true explorers we came ashore in Battery Park, South Manhattan, the territory of what was previously known as New Amsterdam. Slowly we made our way to the most northerly point of Manhattan. You are not likely to find tourists

Foreword

there. Along the way we came across well-known and lesser-known monuments, museums, shops, music clubs, restaurants, and many more remarkable places. We ended in Inwood Hill Park, where we even found the secret spot, the locals say, where Manhattan was bought from the Native Americans. We were constantly being surprised. This is Manhattan! A stretched-out primeval forest. Coyotes sneak across the railway bridge from the mountainy wilderness just outside of New York. We even crept in caves where the Native Americans once lived.

Our thanks go out to all who contributed to the construction of this book. We would also like to thank our nearest family members, and enthusiastic New York visitors, Yvonne, Evelien, Sonja, Frank, and Ferry. They certainly helped us with our research. We still owe them a cronut, the current taste sensation of New York that is, of course, also discussed in this book. We hope that *The Enchantment of New York* is a useful, beautiful, and pleasant book for you.

—Willem Post, The Hague

Introduction

F. Scott Fitzgerald wrote in *The Great Gatsby*:

"The city seen from the Queensboro Bridge is always the city seen for the first time, in its wild promise of all the mystery and the beauty in the world."

"You know, I should have been born in New York, man. I should have been born in the Village! That's where I belong."
—John Lennon, 1970

New York. City of superlatives. Twenty-eight thousand restaurants, fourteen thousand yellow cabs, the legal, and the much more illegal. We have asked many of our compatriots what they think is so magical about New York. In our country, this question was often met with a reply such as "Don't be so silly" followed by a smile on their face. Sparkling eyes. Even a look that resembled falling in love. An exclamation, a cry: "Totally amazing," "What a city," or "I want to visit it straight away!" This love affair is so self-evident that people often only need to use very few words. New York? "It says it all!"

With this book we want to take a shot at making the magic of New York tangible and visible. What sets this city apart is the enormous amount of diversity. No New Yorker can claim that their ethnic group or religion is the most prominent of this city. Diversity enables creativity. All those cultures are squished together in one territory in Manhattan, a relatively small area. Something special is bound to be birthed there. It sure is busy, but the essence of Manhattan allows for its inhabitants to treasure and embrace their own individuality: Chinatown, Little Italy, Koreatown, Little Brazil, Harlem, Spanish Harlem, and so on and so forth. We even discovered traces of Klein Deutschland in the streets between the Upper East Side and Carl Schurz Park. There is an almost endless range of cultures.

This colorful diversity allows for everyone to be themselves like in no other city in the world. Whoever visits New York experiences a sense of freedom. New Yorkers are not often surprised. John Lennon noticed this when he moved in with Yoko Ono. In the song "New York City," the follow-up to "Imagine," he shouted:

"Well, nobody came to bug us, hustle us, or shove us
So we decided to make it our home.
If the Man wants to shove us out, we gonna jump and shout
The Statue of Liberty said, 'Come!'"

New York, despite the tragedy of 9/11, has become more popular than ever. The hotels are packed full, and Times Square seems even busier than before. Susan Wall, the vice president of NYC & Company, the convention and visitors bureau, says: "New York City is the place where the world does business. We are the capital of the media, the publishing firms, the entertainment industry, the fashion industry, and the financial services. Our international gatherings break all visitor records."

But still, what exactly is the magic of New York? What makes New York the city of all cities? There will always be an indefinable quality to that magic. Something like a feeling that you can't bring to words. Or, as Simone de Beauvoir put it:

"There is something in the New York air that makes sleep useless."

New Yorkers are not humble, but how could they be? To survive in this city with its murderous competition in every corner of the market, one must be made of stainless steel and must passionately believe in oneself. Those who really want to get to know New York should visit Donald Trump's golden towers on Fifth Avenue near Central Park, but also slip down to the Lower East Side to see the different faces of the city of the past and the present.

The Lower East Side, with its new galleries and boutiques, is very up-and-coming. You can still see how it was a rough and poor neighborhood when visiting areas near Orchard Street. This is where you will find the typical apartment blocks with iron fire escapes. Now trendy, these used to be a sign of pure poverty. The Tenement Museum is, in fact, partly still one of those original tenement buildings that housed poor immigrants from the nineteenth century, but has been left completely intact. Up to twenty-five poverty-stricken people used to sleep in one room.

The Lower East Side was not the only place stricken by poverty. Down south near where Chinatown currently sits lies the atmospheric Columbus Park where hundreds of Chinese families come to play cards and other games. But in the nineteenth

century, this area was almost hell on earth, and displayed the most poignant forms of poverty imaginable. Charles Dickens visited the Five Points here, the prominent slum district of the known world, and was astonished at what he saw:

"From every corner, as you glance about you in these dark retreats, some figure crawls half-awakened, as if the judgment-hour were near at hand, and every obscene grave were giving up its dead. Where dogs would howl to lie, women, and men, and boys slink off to sleep, forcing the dislodged rats to move away in quest of better lodgings."

A city of contrasts. This, especially, is what makes the city so interesting. The sweet song "*White Christmas*" by Irving Berlin makes winter in New York even more magical than the city already is with its Christmas trees, Saks, Macy's, and all the other shops on Fifth and Madison, luxurious Christmas shop windows. This is the same city in which Berlin, a poor immigrant child from Russia, grew up. He never forgot his heritage and he said:

"Everybody ought to have a Lower East Side in their life."

This rawness is certainly from New York. New York is a cathartic city. He who wants to go forward here *can*, nay, must, work hard. New York attracts a lot of young people. The bars and restaurants are filled with people in their twenties and thirties. The

city is teeming with students and artists who come to the city for its intellectual and cultural climate, and its many well-respected schools. In Chelsea alone, there are hundreds of art exhibitions. In 1964, the writer Hans Habe was surprised about how self-evident it is for New Yorkers to make use of the cultural offerings of the city. He visited a concert, of the world-renowned Pablo Casals, in the conference hall of the United Nations where the politicians and diplomats gathered:

"The hall was filled with students, New York ladies, music lovers, black intellectuals—and in unusual places a few diplomats. No one, or nearly no one, was "dressed"; most of the gentlemen were in walking outfits, the people had coats and fur coats laid on their laps, almost as if they came for a film viewing. It was this informality that gave the afternoon its seriousness. In New York, you get used to the unusual. I got the feeling as if these two thousand people, after the concert, would continue on, to another show, perhaps, and from there to another play or reading. And not just these two thousand people. Half of New York seemed uninterruptedly on their way from plays to concerts, from operas to debates . . . In New York, the culture dresses itself not in her Sunday best, but her progressive overalls."

"A city on the move." A mass of people like an anthill in the concrete jungle. Champagne is being popped at Times Square. I can't think of a single place on this earth where the senses tingle

THE ENCHANTMENT OF NEW YORK

as much as they do here. There is a cacophony of traffic but also a sense of quiet in the parks. The Ravine of Central Park makes you long for the valleys in Austria.

February 1966 was the first time that I fully came into contact with the phenomenon that is New York City. As a Dutch commentator on US affairs of Dutch television, I worked with the master of television story telling, and journalist, Cees Overgauw on a program called *Hollanders in New York*. Amazing! We traveled through the whole city. We spoke with a black mayor, David Dinkins, but also with the Holland Dames, New York's aristocratic ladies whose heritage runs back to the first generation of Dutchmen, who, overall, had it pretty good. What a breathtaking view from the Waldorf Astoria! We were surprised at all of the Dutch influences. We spoke to Charles Gehring, a German American scientist from the New Netherlands Institute who studies the history of the city and its Dutch influences. New York and Amsterdam look like each other. "Every time I walk out of Amsterdam Central Station, I feel like I'm in New York. The diversity, the atmosphere." Gehring also told us that "all American schoolbooks should be rewritten, because it was definitely not the British who were responsible for the tolerance and freedom that we see in the current New York, it was the Dutch."

All of this allows for a better understanding of why Amsterdam felt so involved, and why it played such an important role at the celebration of New York's four hundredth anniversary in 2009 (in 1609, Henry Hudson sailed in service of the United East India Company on the *Halve Maen* to America). What's remarkable is that other Dutch cities also have this bond with New York; which they cherish and proudly mirror the American metropolis. Rotterdam has a famous Hotel New York, and before this the city had the Wilhelminakade from which many Dutch people made the trip to America. The Holland-America line is an understanding of both sides of the Atlantic Ocean. The *SS Rotterdam* still lies in the harbor of the city and because

of Rotterdam's impressive skyline it's referred to as "Manhattan on the Maas."

The Hague is known as the "City of Peace and Justice." New York's secretary-general of the United Nations, Ban Ki-moon, on the hundredth anniversary of the Vredespaleis called it "the epicenter of international law and accountability." New York is the *political* heart of the United Nations, The Hague is the *legal* heart. This same Vredespaleis was built thanks to a large financial donation from philanthropist and peace activist Andrew Carnegie, whose mansion at Central Park is now an interesting museum and of course holds a place as one of the seventy-five attractions in this book. On our explorations of New York we discovered that until 1975 there was a Hague Street

the city a few weeks after this incident, amid all its solemnity. But even then, there was still a sense of typical New York humor. Right near the smoking mess of Ground Zero, a large sign was erected that read, "Bin Laden missed us," with an arrow pointing to the entrance of a bar.

right near the Brooklyn Bridge. A school was built and thus the street is no longer in existence. This school reached all news centers in 1850 because of a huge explosion at residences numbered three and five, which resulted in sixty-seven people losing their lives.

The Dutch feel connected to this city that carries its blue and orange colors on its city arms, and has many Dutch street names. The city that used to be called New Amsterdam set up a parliament with laws that worked themselves up the democratic chain of command of the United States.

New York's famous tolerance policies should be understood according to historical proceedings. The board of New Amsterdam certainly allowed for religious freedom, but this tolerance was limited to the sitting rooms of those religious people. There was an understanding that despite any religious background one might have, one should still be able to do business with another. Alas, due to this salesman mentality, neither New Amsterdam nor New York could get away from the scourge of slavery. New York attributes its tolerant character in large degree to its current inhabitants. The Big Apple is a magnet and attracts all kinds of free-spirited people. It's unbelievable how the city blossomed after the tragedy of 9/11. That unbreakable resilience! I visited

As of yet, we have not answered the question of what the enchantment of New York really is. New York is an amazing city that you must discover for yourself. That discovery starts in Manhattan, and we are confident that the seventy-five places we have written down for you will help you find the answer. As far as we are concerned, you can start your journey right now. This is a nice moment to listen to the first sentences of the immortal song "New York, New York" by Frank Sinatra:

"Start spreadin' the news
I'm leaving today
I want to be a part of it
New York, New York.
These vagabond shoes
Are longing to stray
Right through the very heart of it
New York, New York."

In Piet Mondriaan's Footsteps

Greenwich Village is a low-rise valley, squished between the skyscrapers of New York. Wide avenues cross many small streets. I naughtily cross 7th Avenue in the middle of the block, instead of the assigned crosswalk. Yellow cabs come straight at me. For a minute, I am Piet, who tried to tame these streets in the 1940s. He consciously crossed the streets very slowly and in that way tried to control the traffic. Absurd, of course, but creating order amongst chaos was his *leitmotiv*. On this cold winter night I'm searching for Mondriaan's spirit. Our freedom fighter escaped fascism, even when Hitler's bombs almost got him as the windows of his London home and studio were smashed out. He had to come from somewhere. He conquered his seasickness in 1940, and traveled to New York, where he moved into the chic Upper East Side. All the traditional music

clubs and theaters can be found there. This is far from the Village, where the homeless, students, and bohemians controlled the atmosphere. It was a cultural free state that the elite stuck their noses up to. He received a record player from his friend Harry Holtzman on which he would play new music such as the boogie-woogie and the blues. The Village in the forties was filled with music clubs and small avant-garde theaters. The 55 Bar and piano bar Marie's Crisis are still there along with countless gay bars. But I am searching for the most special one of all: the Café Society Club on Sheridan Square numbers one and two. Barney Josephson opened this place in 1938. He was a simple shoe salesman

Victory Boogie-Woogie—Piet Mondriaan

who had saved up a few dollars to bring his music dream to reality. A small basement was where, for the first time, racial integration was allowed. Black and white artists performed for a mixed audience. Josephson gave his business a chic and satirical name, provoking the upper class. The doorman wore ragged gloves and made the guests step out of the cabs themselves. Inside hung a ripped picture of Hitler, as Billie Holiday sang her world-famous "Strange Fruit" about the lynching in the South. Nights consisted of the constant shift between political satire and boogie-woogie music. On many nights, Piet Mondriaan would travel to the Café Society Club. He danced into the depths of night to the new "free" music. "Enormous, enormous," is what he allegedly would repeat all night. He felt at home here. This rhythm and dynamic is very recognizable in his glorious *Victory Boogie-Woogie* painting.

I'm standing at Sheridan Square. Where is the Café Society Club? The square has changed over time. Old numbers have disappeared. I see an old, white building on the corner with an antique store. I walk in. Was there ever a music club near this place? The young owner of the store looks at me. "Yes, right next door. It's an old theater with a set of stairs that go downward. People rarely go there anymore. Every now and again an old New Yorker comes to me and says there used to be amazing shows played down there." When I walk outside, I notice the faded numbers one and two on the wall. I look inside and see the stairs where Piet, Charlie Chaplin, Eleanor Roosevelt, and all those others wandered down. It didn't end well with the Café Society Club. The club went under when the left-political satire was blacklisted during the Cold War. Yet, the spirit of the Village has remained intact. Jimi Hendrix and Bob Dylan were discovered in this area in the sixties. John Lennon used to live here. Willem de Kooning used to bartend at the Cedar Club. Their spirit, as well as that of Piet Mondriaan, still carries on throughout the Village. Uninterrupted.

Atelier in New York

"Victory Boogie-Woogie" - Piet Mondriaan

The 1944 painting is considered to be the most important modern painting about New York, and alongside Picasso's *Guernica* and Warhol's *Campbell's Soup Cans* it is considered to be one of the most important works of art of the twentieth century. The piece is primarily painted in the three primary colors blue, yellow, and red, as they dance around each other in sets of small squares. This appeals to the free "boogie-woogie jazz" music that was all the rage in New York during wartimes. This painting exudes the dynamic of New York. The Dutchman Mondriaan, who as an artist escaped fascist Europe to the free New York, considered this painting the successor to his own *Broadway Boogie-Woogie* from 1942–43. The word "victory" refers to the triumph of free art in these dark times. Barack Obama visited The Hague on March 25, 2014, in accordance with the Nuclear Security Summit. After the summit, the president visited the painting in the Municipal museum of The Hague. He was thoroughly impressed: "This is a fabulous one." President Obama promised to return to this beautiful museum once again with his family. The Municipal of The Hague is established in one of the most beautiful art-deco buildings. This museum has the largest Mondriaan collection in the world.

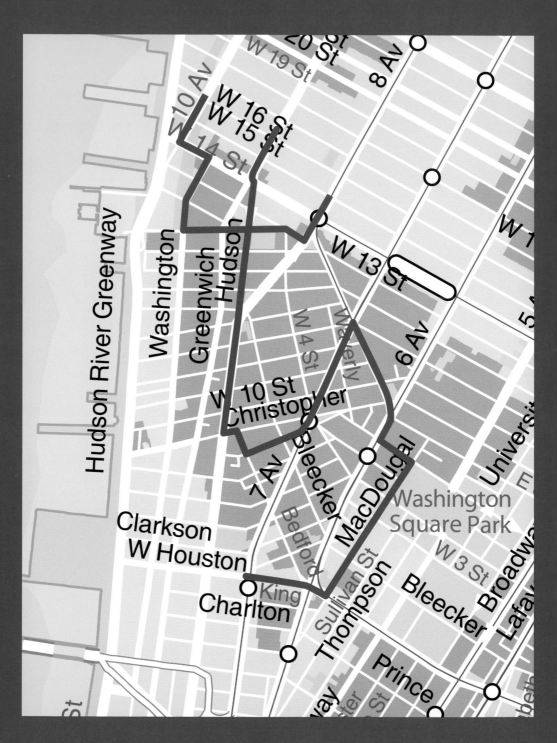

Walk 1: **West Village, Meatpacking.**
The Sixties "Revisited"

DURATION: LARGE PORTION OF THE DAY

Step off subway line 1 onto the Houston Street/Varick Street station.

Walk east across West Houston Street. From here, cross 6th Avenue and take your first left onto MacDougal Street. At this point, you are essentially walking straight into the sixties. Number 94 is where Bob Dylan moved in, in 1969. At number 115, you will find Café Wha?, where Dylan first performed on a cold winter's day and left his proverbial footprint in the Village. This is also Jimi Hendrix's home base. At number 116 is the Gaslight Café and the Kettle of Fish. Allen Ginsberg created poetry in the Gaslight. Dylan also visited here frequently. At number 124 is the Grove Bar, a famous bar from the sixties that is around the corner from an **amazing mural** 32. At 129, you will find a lovely Italian restaurant called **La Lanterna di Vittorio** 33. Now, continue walking and on the right side you will find **Washington Square**. The fountain and the bow are real eye-catchers 34. When you arrive at Waverly Place, take a left. On the right you will pass Washington Square Hotel. Across the street is where First Lady Eleanor Roosevelt had an apartment. On the left you will pass the famous restaurant Babbo, where Tony Soprano often got off his scooter to greet his friend Mario Batali. Take a right on 6th Avenue; continue walking until you reach America's oldest pharmacy, **C. O. Bigelow** at 414 6th Avenue 36. From there, walk back a little bit on 6th Avenue and cross onto Greenwich Avenue and walk until you reach 7th Avenue. Take a left; walk to Sheridan Square where you will find **the Gay Liberation Monument** 37. The Stonewall Inn is where the world-famous gay emancipation movement took place. This area is filled with music clubs such as the **55 Bar** 38. Cross 7th Avenue and walk on to Grove Street. To the right you will see **Marie's Crisis** piano bar and **Arthur's Tavern** 39 (if you're here at night it is definitely worth visiting the intimate and excellent Small's jazz club at 183 West 10th Street).

Walk along Grove Street. On the corner of Bedford Street is a lovely restaurant named Little Owl. The apartment above this restaurant is where the sitcom *Friends* was filmed. Walk via Bedford Street, one of the most beautiful places in the Village, to Hudson Street. You can rest for a while in the **Garden of St. Luke in the Fields** Church 40. From here, walk north up Hudson Street for approximately half an hour—it eventually becomes 9th Avenue. Here you will find the **Chelsea Market** at number 75 44. You can walk straight through this former cookie factory via the main entrance. As you exit the back way you will notice a flight of stairs on your right to the **High Line** 43. Walk south along these old rails. The High Line ends in the **Meatpacking District**. Here you will find many a fine restaurant for lunch or dinner 45. The Gansevoort Hotel is a landmark with a unique roof terrace. At the crossing of 8th Avenue and West 14th Street is a subway station with lines A, C, and E.

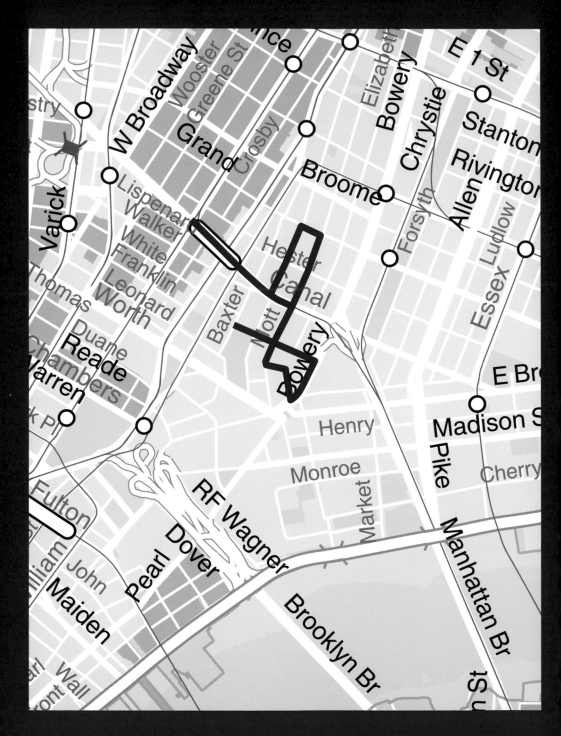

Walk 2: **Chinatown, Little Italy.**
A World of Scent, Color, and Tastes

DURATION: APPROXIMATELY THREE HOURS

Start on Canal Street. Note: This long and busy street has multiple subway stations.

As you step out on the corner of Broadway, Lafayette Street, or Centre Street, walk east on Canal Street. This has always been known as the place for cheap street trading. On the left, you will see the Baxter and Walker Street crossing at the red information shop. Continue walking and take a right onto Mott Street. Soon you will see the **Ten Ren** tea shop at number 75 `15`. Cross the street; as you pass a few stores you will find a Buddhist temple at number 64. You can walk inside and take in the scent of incense. Continue walking along Mott Street and take a right on Bayard Street. After a minute of walking you will arrive in the atmospheric **Columbus Park** `12` (near here you will find the **Night Court** `11`). Walk back again and turn right onto Mott Street. At number 65 is the oldest tenement building of New York, built in 1824. Many poor immigrants used to be packed into one of these rooms, very degrading circumstances. Take a left on Pell Street and walk up to **Doyer Street**—You are now standing at a historically daunting crossing `13`. If you would like to eat something, you will find Joe's Shanghai at number 9 Pell Street. The pork or crab soup dumplings are a delicacy. Walk along Doyer Street, a windy barber street, and take a left into the Bowery. Soon you will see Bayard Street, at which point you want to take a left. At number 65 is the famous **Chinatown Ice Cream Factory**, a small business with delicious ice cream `14`.

From here, walk to the crossing and take a right onto Mott Street. Cross Canal Street and continue walking along Mott Street for quite some time until you reach the Grand Street crossing. This last area is known for its fish, herb, vegetable, and fruit markets. Sometimes you might come across live produce such as frogs in a bucket. Turn left onto Grand Street and you will discover another world: Little Italy! At 195 Grand Street there is the bakery and lunchroom Ferrara, which since 1892 has created the most delicious pastry: cannoli. Turn left onto Mulberry Street and you will find yourself amongst countless restaurants that have lovely terraces open when the weather is nice. At the end of the street, right near the Canal Street crossing, you will see the **Most Precious Blood Church** `16`. As you exit the church, go right. From Mulberry Street you should walk to the right onto Canal Street and on to the subway stations. Our recommendation is to certainly visit the Museum of Chinese in America at 215 Centre Street, just to the right of Canal Street. This is an interesting display of history, and was designed by Maya Lin, who also created the Vietnam Monument in Washington. The museum is closed on Tuesday and Wednesday.

Walk 3: Lower East Side, East Village. History, Art, and Trendy Shopping

DURATION: APPROXIMATELY FOUR HOURS

From the Delancy Street–Essex Street subway station (lines F, J, M, and Z) it is a fifteen-minute walk to the **Tenement Museum**. Turn left at the Orchard Street crossing and you will instantly see 103 Orchard Street. This remarkable museum building still has the original sleeping places of the poor immigrants from the nineteenth century **17**. It is smart to visit www.tenement.org to reserve tours and tickets beforehand.

In the Lower East Side, the once poverty-stricken neighborhood, you will now find dozens of restaurants and bars such as the Orchard Street Café Dancer at number 96 and the Gallery Bar at number 120. **Art galleries** have sprung up like mushrooms across the area **19**. Walk along Orchard Street until you reach East Houston Street. Take a right on East Houston Street and walk for about a minute until you reach number 205. Here, you will find **Katz's Deli**, which serves a unique culinary experience, such as the pastrami sandwich **27**. Walk back along East Houston Street, past Orchard Street, and at number 179 is the historical and atmospheric Russ & Daughters, who specialize in caviar, smoked fish, herring, and of course bagels. This is your best opportunity to come eat a real Dutch herring. Keep walking along East Houston Street, turn right onto 1st Avenue, and enter the trendy East Village. Turn left onto 2nd Street. Cross 2nd Avenue, and at number 2 on 2nd Street is **John Derian**'s famous interior paradise **28**. Walk along Bond Street, the extension of 2nd Street, and you will enter the most trendy fashion streets of New York. At number 57 on the left is **Curve**, one of the highest fashion businesses for men and women in the United States **29**. A little farther on, on the same side, is United Nude at number 25, who have a very eye-catching shoe collection. On the opposite side of the street you will find the clothing shop Oak, known for their ultra-hip, avant-garde clothing for men and women. They are also known for their shoes and jewelry. Continue walking and turn left onto Lafayette Street, which will lead you back to East Houston Street. Walk back again in the direction of Russ & Daughters and turn via Lafayette Street onto the first side street: Elizabeth Street, one of the trendiest shopping streets. At number 267, on the right, is **Tacombi**, the remarkable Mexican restaurant that has a Volkswagen van in the center of it **22**. Very close, on the same side of the street, you will find **Dolce Vita** for shoes and fashion at number 255 **21**. At number 233 is Le Labo, an extremely popular store with the most delightful scents and perfumes. Around the corner at 17 Prince Street is La Habana, known for their grilled corn. At 173 Elizabeth Street you can buy special jewelry at Erica Weiner. Turn after the Bowery. Across the street you will see the remarkable **New Museum** at number 235 **20**. There are multiple subway stations in the area, for example at Bowery-Delancey Street (J and Z lines).

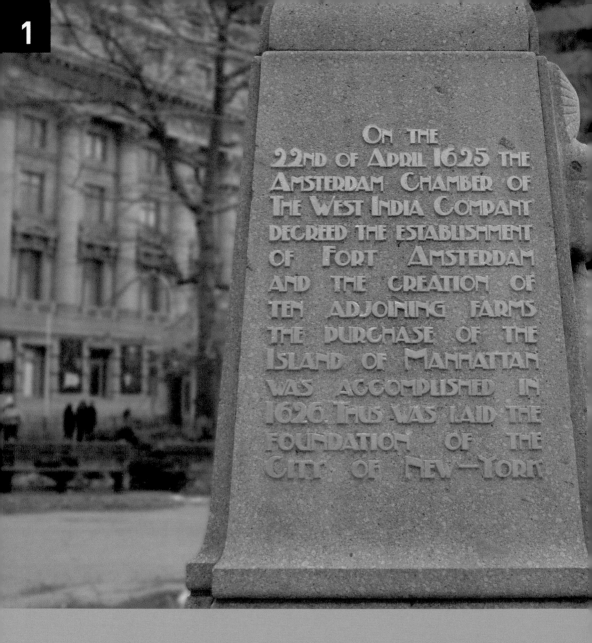

On the 22nd of April 1625 the Amsterdam Chamber of the West India Company decreed the establishment of Fort Amsterdam and the creation of ten adjoining farms the purchase of the island of Manhattan was accomplished in 1626 thus was laid the foundation of the city of New-York.

1

The Netherlands Monument

BATTERY PARK

At the entrance of the northeast side of Battery Park is the monumental art-deco flagstaff that was offered by the Dutch on December 6, 1926, to the city of New York "as a mark of a century-old and unbroken friendship." The Netherlands was the first country that acknowledged the United States. The first foreign salute was from "our" St. Eustatius on November 6, 1776, to the American ship the *Andrew Doria*, which had the Declaration of Independence aboard.

The bottom part of the monument that is made of granite was designed by a sculptor from Harlem named Hendrik van den Eijnde. The first blueprint of New Amsterdam was etched into this platform. The monument displays Peter Minuit, the man who bought the land from the Native Americans. The inscription states that the Amsterdam Chamber of the West India Company affirmed the sale. "Amsterdam" was assigned to build Fort Amsterdam, which is across from the current monument, on April 22, 1625. From the monument there is a magnificent view of the river, which is named after the English Captain Henry Hudson, who sailed the Dutch ship *De Halve Maen* on this river. The journey was assigned by the United East India Company to search for new possible sailing routes to China.

Accessibility

4 **5** Bowling Green

R Whitehall Street

2

Fraunces Tavern

**54 PEARL STREET, CORNER OF BROAD STREET,
FINANCIAL DISTRICT/WALL STREET**

In the shadow of the forest of skyscrapers in South Manhattan, is the tavern named after its eighteenth-century owner Samuel Fraunces. In this smoky tavern is where the American revolutionaries gathered and organized a tea party, just like in Boston, against the British governmental bodies who wanted to raise the tax in the area. In the "long room" on the upper level you can still stand on the spot where George Washington said good-bye to his officers at the end of the American War of Independence. New York was the first capital city of the independent United States. The ministry of foreign affairs was initially established in the Fraunces Tavern.

Traditional-styled dining is still available today. Washington's favorite dish, chicken potpie, a hearty tart filled with chicken, is very popular. There is also a range of Irish beers and whiskeys available. Those who wish to dive into a piece of history should visit the upper level. In the museum upstairs you can marvel at the lock of hair and real tooth of America's first president.

According to the Sons of the Revolution, this historic building is the oldest property in New York.

Accessibility

 Whitehall Street

3

Charging Bull

1 BOWLING GREEN, LOWER MANHATTAN

Suddenly, there it was. Next to the large Christmas tree across from the stock market on Wall Street. A giant bronze bull that artist Arturo Di Modica had been working on for two years, and which cost him $300,000 to create. In utter secrecy the bull had been brought from Brooklyn to Manhattan on the early morning of December 15, 1989. Di Modica wanted to play Santa Claus for a day and gift the people this bull after the stock market crisis of 1987. He called the secret operation a form of guerilla art. This piece of art had to symbolize power, optimism, and thus recovery. The bull was seized by the police within twenty-four hours, but thanks to the massive attention it got from the press, the bull found a safe spot in Bowling Green Park. When the Occupy Wall Street protesters continuously started to gather around near the bull, a powerful symbol of capitalism, it soon received police protection, 24/7, for several weeks. The protesters later revealed they were not aiming their protest at the bull. For many visitors, the bull seems to carry a magical property: the nose, horns, and genitals are very polished from all the people touching it. Many movie directors in Hollywood and Bollywood are grateful for the bull. It weighs close to 7,055 pounds and is over sixteen feet tall. Di Modica often walks past his bull and is said to be very humbled by the popularity of his Christmas gift. More bulls are on the agenda. There is already another bull in Shanghai, and in July 2012 another was spontaneously placed on the Beursplein in Amsterdam, with the purpose of giving Europe an optimistic boost with regard to the solution of the economic crisis that this part of the world had been affected by—thus, a very generous giver.

Accessibility

 Bowling Green Station

4

FDNY Memorial Wall

**124 LIBERTY STREET, CORNER OF GREENWICH STREET,
FINANCIAL DISTRICT**

Fire Station 10, "The Ten House," stands on the edge of Ground Zero. When the towers collapsed on September 11, 2001, many tons of rubble and other material fell onto this building. The windows and a large part of the interior were blown away. Five firefighters from this station were found dead. The nearest lawyers' office Holland & Knight lost a volunteer firefighter, Glenn Winuk. Glenn rushed out of the office to help those in need. To remember his heroic deed, his colleagues organized a collection service for the monument and all 343 affected firefighters were to be honored. The bronze accents designed by Rambusch Company in 2006 display their rescue mission. Beneath them reads the following:

Dedicated to those who fell and to those who carry on. May we never forget.

Fellow firefighters wrote personal messages on the back of the plaque "that shall be kept for eternity" in the presence of President Bush. All of the names of the firefighters who died have been engraved. Next of kin can make paper copies of this.

Accessibility

R   Cortlandt Street

5

Century 21

22 CORTLANDT STREET, FINANCIAL DISTRICT

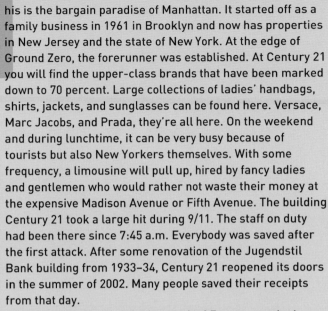

This is the bargain paradise of Manhattan. It started off as a family business in 1961 in Brooklyn and now has properties in New Jersey and the state of New York. At the edge of Ground Zero, the forerunner was established. At Century 21 you will find the upper-class brands that have been marked down to 70 percent. Large collections of ladies' handbags, shirts, jackets, and sunglasses can be found here. Versace, Marc Jacobs, and Prada, they're all here. On the weekend and during lunchtime, it can be very busy because of tourists but also New Yorkers themselves. With some frequency, a limousine will pull up, hired by fancy ladies and gentlemen who would rather not waste their money at the expensive Madison Avenue or Fifth Avenue. The building Century 21 took a large hit during 9/11. The staff on duty had been there since 7:45 a.m. Everybody was saved after the first attack. After some renovation of the Jugendstil Bank building from 1933–34, Century 21 reopened its doors in the summer of 2002. Many people saved their receipts from that day.

Those who haven't had enough of *Zagat* magazine's number-one bargain store of New York can catch bus 111 or 114 from the Port Authority Bus Terminal to the Jersey Gardens Mall, the largest mall of New Jersey. Even there you will find sales at stores such as Abercrombie & Fitch. As a tourist you will hardly have to pay any tax on these goods. A return ticket will cost you about $13. The bus station is on the corner of 42nd Street–8th Avenue. For this visit you will need at least half a day.

Accessibility

R   Cortlandt Street

6

Irish Hunger Memorial

CORNER OF VESEY STREET AND NORTH END AVENUE, BATTERY PARK

Around this terrain, brought over from Ireland, you will find stones, earth, and vegetation of West Ireland. This emotionally heavy monument was erected in memory of the one million people who died as a result of the Great Irish Potato Famine. As you walk through the hall you will hear Irish music and voices telling you about the great despair these Irish American people wished to escape. One of the engravings reads: "They are dying as numerous as bees on a harvest day, burying them in their own clothes, without a coffin or any other thing requisite for them to defray their funeral charges." Eight hundred thousand of New York's current inhabitants have an Irish background.

Accessibility

 World Trade Center

7

Cycling across the Brooklyn Bridge

PARK ROW, ACROSS FROM CITY HALL

You will notice it right away. You can rent a bicycle in many places in New York—it seems like a bicycle revolution. This is in the notion of health and durability! Reliable bicycles can be hired via www. bikeandroll.com. The easiest pickup location of this company's bicycles is in Battery Park, though you could also pick your bicycle up from Pier 84 at the Hudson River, but you would have to cross through Manhattan. You cycle for twenty minutes to the driveway of the Brooklyn Bridge. It opened in 1883 and until 1903 was the largest bridge in the world. At the time there was some worry that the bridge might collapse in on itself. Six days after the opening twelve people died at the crossing after a panic frenzy. It wasn't until 1884, when a ringmaster tested if twenty-two elephants could cross the bridge, that the public was reassured about the bridge's safety. There is also a Dutch plaque on the bridge: *Eendragt maakt Magt* (Unity creates Strength). From essentially any spot on the bridge you will have a beautiful view of Manhattan. Lovers attach a padlock to the bridge and throw the key in the water below as a sign of their eternal bond. For the return trip, plus a few photo ops, you will need a few hours. You can also hire a guide.

Accessibility

J **Z** Chambers Street

6 Brooklyn Bridge/City Hall

8

African Burial Ground

CORNER OF DUANE STREET AND ELK STREET,
LOWER MANHATTAN

Even though New Amsterdam, now New York, is known for its relatively tolerant character, Dutch and British traders often brought slaves to shore. Nearly half of the households had slaves in 1703. For these slaves there was a separate burial ground outside of the walls of New Amsterdam.

A piece of forgotten history. In 1991, the remains of the bodies were found at the building site of a new skyscraper, leading to lots of extreme emotions. After some research of the bone remains, it was discovered that the slaves were malnourished and abused. President Bush appointed this site the 123rd national monument of the United States in 2006. In the place of the burial site a large sunken space was created where people now gather to remember this part of history. There is a map of Africa and of the United States engraved on the ground. The people were reburied and the story of the Open Door was told. Whoever went from Africa through this door never came back. The stones of the monument are from South Africa and North America. It is an impressive place to visit.

On one of the walls the following words have been engraved:

For all those who were lost,
For all those who were stolen,
For all those who were left behind,
For all those who were not forgotten.

Accessibility

R City Hall

4 **5** **6** Brooklyn Bridge/ City Hall

9

Steven Alan Annex

103 FRANKLIN STREET, TRIBECA

Why is this clothing store for men and women so popular? The answer is simple: here you will find the latest trends for a reasonable price. Steven Alan clothing is known for its impressive colors and its original prints, from the large range of denim jeans to the cool tops and T-shirts. You can even buy a nice cocktail dress here. This business is very loved in the neighborhood and gives its stylish clientele the impression that they belong here. Steven Alan stays true to the small design labels such as Isabel Marant, A. P. C., Sessun, and Nice Collective. Jewelry, bags, and beauty products are also sold here. From time to time they offer interesting sales. Something remarkable is the installation behind the counter from which music such as Velvet Underground, Elvis Costello, and Led Zeppelin can be heard.

You can find other Steven Alan complexes around New York, but this one holds our preference. This is thanks to the enthusiastic staff. Since you're there anyway, you might as well visit number 158 for the various collections of accessories at the Steven Alan Home Shop.

steven alan

Accessibility

 Franklin Street

10

Cortlandt Alley Museum

BETWEEN FRANKLIN STREET AND WHITE STREET, TRIBECA

Welcome to the smallest museum in the world, built in an abandoned lift shaft. The museum is the property of the production company Red Bucket Films. This nonprofit museum aims to collect objects that have been taken out of context. According to one of the young founders of the museum, Alex Kalman, people are often aware of the absurdity, beauty, or ugliness, and thus understand the deeper meaning of everyday objects. There is a collection of objects that were found in old copiers, but also an interesting collection of toothpaste tubes from all over the world donated by the industrial designer Tucker Viemeister. In a see-through plastic box is a shoe that allegedly belonged to an Iraqi journalist who threw his shoe at President Bush in 2008. There is also a short piece of barbed wire, which came from a concentration camp in Dachau. The exhibition of a collection of chip packets from all over the world also draws people's attention. A school lesson about the world's cultures was given as a response to this collection. The exhibitions are constantly changing. The museum is open seven days a week, meaning you can look through the window or the keyhole. You can only really go in on the weekends, but then it's only open to about three people at a time. It's possible you might see a guide sitting outside on a chair having his lunch. A Nespresso coffee machine and a dish of biscuits can be found in the café, and one shelf of T-shirts can be found in the gift shop.

Accessibility

 Canal Street

 Canal Street

11

Night Court

100 CENTRE STREET, CHINATOWN

The city that never sleeps placed an evening and even a night court into effect in response to the *lik op stuk* policy (tit-for-tat policy). You are welcome to enter from six until one o'clock. You will have to make your way through the security gates. You must follow the instructions ensuring that you are not allowed to have any form of weapon and your cell phone must be turned off. It's a most fascinating display, though the spectacles you might see on television don't always walk past. Generally, suspects who have been arrested throughout the day are led through the court wearing handcuffs. Ninety-five percent of the people are assigned a lawyer from Legal Aid. The cases mostly consist of petty thefts, drug abuse, and drug trafficking. The lawyer and the accused go back and forth before the judge announces his verdict. There are many alternative forms of punishment. "Next!" For foreigners, the Night Court is a strange phenomenon, but also presents an overview of the American judicial system and all of its ins and outs. It also presents a sense of what happens behind the scenes of the concrete jungle. The Night Court doesn't only affect anonymous New Yorkers; even Jennifer Lopez and Tupac Shakur have been brought in.

Accessibility

(**J**) Chambers Street

(**4**) (**6**) Brooklyn Bridge/ City Hall

12

Columbus Park

**67 MULBERRY STREET, BETWEEN BAYARD STREET
AND WORTH STREET, CHINATOWN**

Where is the most cultural place in Chinatown? Columbus Park! At stone tables Chinese Americans often play chess or mahjong in small groups. Others participate in yoga and tai chi exercises. Often you can also hear Chinese music, performed by street performers. Fortune-tellers predict the future. The park opened in 1897 and is the creation of Calvert Vaux, co-designer of Central Park. The place carries a peaceful atmosphere. It is bizarre to realize that Columbus Park was settled in the nineteenth century on the place of the notorious Five Points slum city. Twenty-five people often stayed in one room in these poverty-stricken living areas.

Herbert Asbury tells a story of a little girl who was murdered on one of these blocks for begging for a penny in his book *The Gangs of New York* (1928). Her body was in the room for five days until her mother buried her in a hole in the floor. Five Points is known as a slum city where more people were murdered than anywhere else in the

world. The area was inhabited by many poor Irish, Italian, and Jewish immigrants, and in 1864 more than eighty thousand people were arrested, then 10 percent of New York's population. There was rubbish everywhere. The water was unclean. Gangs such as the "Bowery Boys" ruled the area. The new Columbus Park was an oasis in an otherwise poverty-stricken neighborhood. At the turn of the century is when many of the Chinese moved into the area.

Accessibility

J Chambers Street

4 **6** Brooklyn Bridge/ City Hall

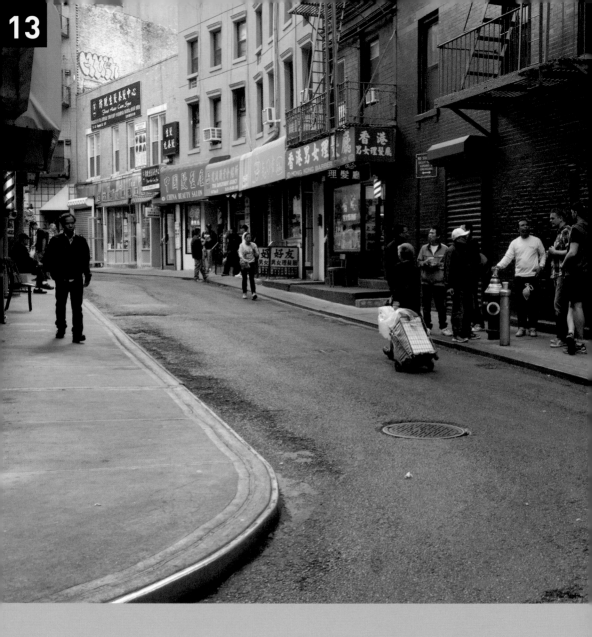

13

Bloody Angle

DOYERS STREET, CHINATOWN

This street in the heart of Chinatown is named after the Dutchman Hendrik Doyer, who, as an immigrant in the eighteenth century, owned a brewery. In those days Doyers Street acted as a cart trail to the brewery. Around the year 1900, more and more Chinese immigrants started to establish themselves in the area. Especially men came together in this narrow, windy street to discuss the latest news from China and to leave letters and money for the home front where new stores started to function as banks and post offices.

Up until the thirties, one bend in Doyers Street was known as the "Bloody Angle." This dark place was the scene for many murders within the criminal circuit, primarily made up of Chinese gangs. Gang members were often shot or caught in a cross fire, which contributed to the fear of the people in the neighborhood. This crime scene was popular amongst murderers because they could flee from the scene very easily. Beneath the street are several secret tunnels and alleyways in accordance with the shops above ground. When passing through Doyers Street, do not forget to visit Ting's gift shop that headlined the news in 1958: twenty-two pounds of heroin were found in the store.

These days, Ting's only sells trinkets and souvenirs. The restaurant the Nom Wah Tea Parlor is famous for its delicious dim sum and its traditionally low prices. This is where these treats were first sold in America. Since 2011, Doyers Street has been well known for its many barbershops. Many immigrants complained to the *New York Times* that Americans don't know how to cut Chinese hair. For that kind of service you should, of course, visit Chinatown.

Accessibility

J N Q

4 6 Canal Street

14

Voted Best Ice Cream in NYC by Citysearch

The Original
**Chinatown
Ice Cream Factory**
華埠雪糕行

New York Chinatown
65 Bayard Street
New York, New York 10013
212.608.4170 | 757.752.8696

Philip Seid
Christina S

www.chinatownicecreamfactory.com | info@chinatownicecreamfactory.com

Chinatown
Ice Cream Factory

65 BAYARD STREET, CHINATOWN

Where can you get America's most popular dessert with a Chinese twist? The place to be is in a long, narrow room in Chinatown at the Chinese Ice Cream Factory. This small family business offers flavors such as green tea, black sesame, and lychee ice cream. Their ice cream is not cheap, but the scoops are very large. Several cultures claim to have invented ice cream, but this factory holds the trump card. The CICF holds the number-one spot in the FOX News Top Ten of best ice creameries. The taste sensations cannot be denied, though the Big Gay Ice Cream Shop at East 125 7th Street in the East Village is also more than worth a visit. During the first couple of years, the two owners drove their ice cream truck across Manhattan. It became a great success. They are still committed to providing marvelous flavors, such as ice cream with salt, at their regular spot in the city. But, if you ask us, the best flavor is the green tea and cinnamon ice cream that can be found in this little store in Chinatown. The same goes for the almond-cookie ice cream from our grandmother's time.

Accessibility

(J) (N) (Q)

(4) (6) Canal Street

15

Ten Ren Tea

75–79 MOTT STREET, CHINATOWN

The successful family business Ten Ren opened in the early eighties as one of the first teahouses in Los Angeles and San Francisco. Mark and Ellen Lii established Ten Ren in 1984 in New York, and it now is their most important store. They are much appreciated by the Chinese community. Amongst their beautiful décor you can see hundreds of boxes and cylinders of tea. Ginseng (used to fight stress and diabetes) is also sold here. This root, and subsequently the tea, also allegedly reduces a sweet tooth. The staff is remarkably helpful and loves to explain that tea is not necessarily a product, but an ingredient of Chinese culture. They love for others to taste their teas. If asked, you can receive an elaborate explanation of which tea suits you best. Their teas are wrapped as neat little gifts. The owners are proud of the fact that celebrities such as Michael Douglas and President George W. Bush have visited them at Ten Ren. At number 75 you will find Ten Ren's Tea Time and Shop, a modern Chinese teahouse where you can drink their trendy bubble tea. This pastel-colored drink is made up of tea, milk, fruit syrup, and tapioca balls made of cassava. If you shake it, it will create a nice, foamy layer. Green milk and jasmine tea, black tea with peach flavoring, and many other warm and ice-cold drinks are available here.

TenRen's TEA
天仁茶業股份有限公司
TEN REN TEA AND GINSENG CO., INC

* 75 MOTT STREET, NEW YORK, NY 10013
TEL: (212)349-2286 FAX: (212)349-2180

* 79 MOTT STREET, NEW YORK, NY 10013
TEL: (212)732-7178

* 138 LAFAYETTE ST., NEW YORK, NY 10013
TEL:(212)343-8098

WWW.TenRenUSA.Com
TOLL FREE:1-800-292-2049

Accessibility

(J) (N) (Q)

(4) (6) Canal Street

16

The Most Precious Blood Church

109 MULBERRY STREET, LITTLE ITALY

Americans with Italian heritage have a weak spot for this picturesque Roman Catholic church that is settled in the ever-expanding Chinatown. In 1891 it was used by a large and expanding group of Italian immigrants in Lower Manhattan who were not welcomed by other churches in New York and thus had to gather in air-raid shelters. Many inhabitants of Mulberry Street were originally from Naples and surrounding areas, where San Gennaro is their patron saint. As the years went by, San Gennaro became a focal figure in the church, which eventually led to the San Gennaro party in 1929. These days, it has become an annual festival of food and drink that attracts many tourists in September to the streets of Little Italy. The days of gambling in the central square during the festival and handing the profits over to the Genovian mafia are over.

In recent years there have no longer been any weekly traditional Italian celebrations. The church is elaborately decorated with statues, murals, and ceiling portraits of the saints. Many older visitors travel long distances to revisit the church of their childhood.

The small garden at the side of the church is worth the visit alone, as it flourishes with colorful flowers and statues. The church currently has an expanding Vietnamese community and therefore is being used for their weekly rosary sessions as well. The church is still directed by an Italian, Father Fabian Grifone, who was married in this church in 1953.

Accessibility

J **N** **Q**

4 **6** Canal Street

17

Tenement Museum

103 ORCHARD STREET, LOWER EAST SIDE

This museum is a must-see for those who want to learn more about the history of New York. In this original nineteenth-century tenement building you will get a glimpse of the social life of immigrants who often came from Ellis Island to the then poverty-stricken part of New York. Every wave of immigrants crossed through the Lower East Side at some point. In 1860 this place was called Klein Deutschland. Soon the Eastern Europeans and Irish came to live here as well. The economic depression during the 1860s up until the Great Depression seventy years later was central to this area. The museum, also very suitable for children, can only be visited in groups with a guide. This is a great way to acquire a lot of knowledge in a short span of time. Shabby rooms, just as they were, can be extensively explored. Many impressive stories will color your imagination. At least seven thousand immigrants inhabited this building without gas, plumbing, or electricity.

In the backyard everyone had to share the communal toilet. Many tours are offered daily, by expert and enthusiastic guides. One of the most impressive tours is the Hard Times tour. Often many single-parented families lived in one room. The competition to earn money was fierce. At one time, there were hundreds of tailors on one street. It wasn't until after the thirties, the time of President Roosevelt's New Deal, that governments helped those in the area. Whoever could get the papers left the Lower East Side to sit on the next step of the social ladder. This museum shop has a lot of interesting things to offer. There are also several walks throughout the neighborhood.

Accessibility

 Delancey Street

 Essex Street

18

The Back Room Bar

102 NORFOLK STREET, LOWER EAST SIDE

THE BACK ROOM

Psst! Don't be afraid. You are standing in front of the grubby fence between numbers 100 and 104. Where is number 102? There is no clear indication. Something that looks like the entrance to a toy factory—no, bar. A staircase behind the fence leads to a dark alley. Let's take a look anyway. You walk through the alley to a closed door. When you knock on the door, a voice asks you for your password. Don't despair, the door will swing open and you await a great surprise. What a contrast! Inside, you will travel through time. Suddenly, you've landed in the 1920s. You could easily call it a small miracle in the Lower East Side. The band performs swinging music from the twenties. Multiple guests are cloaked in the charming dress of the Roaring Twenties. Even the traditional hairdos play their part. It's as if you're on a film set. It smells like the twenties in this speakeasy, says the doorman. With some perplexity, you will find patrons drinking out of small white coffee cups. But it's not coffee, it's alcohol. This is where The Back Room was settled in the twenties. Due to Prohibition, people often hid their alcoholic drinks in small white coffee cups. There are multiple exits, including the bookcase, and they are not there for nothing. This way, mafia bosses such as Lucky Luciano and Meyer Lansky could flee the scene when the police would raid the joint. This classic, monumental bar is wholly complete. The Back Room is often used in commercials. Oh, and there is a VIP room, but that is only for real gangsters.

Accessibility

 F   Delancey Street

 J   M   Essex Street

19

Orchard Street
Art and Galleries

ORCHARD STREET, LOWER EAST SIDE

aw romance! This seems like a paradox, but Orchard Street has it all—it is still recognizable as the street between Chinatown and East Houston Street, with its eight apartment blocks accompanied by steel fire escapes. From the nineteenth century until just recently, this was a rough street with lots of poor immigrants. First, there was Klein Deutschland. Then came the Irish, the Eastern Europeans, the Italians, and later the Chinese. Now, it is a street of total diversity where many people from the middle class establish themselves. The fabric and other specialty stores are slowly being swapped out for luxurious boutiques and art galleries. Our favorites? At number 27, the Strange Loop Gallery, run by Alesia Exum from New York and Claire Fleury from Amsterdam. In this popular gallery you will find clothing, photographs, paintings, and films. The vintage exterior alone is pure art. Media such as the *Washington Post*, the *New York Times*, and *Newsweek* have given attention to Strange Loop.

At number 98, Castle Fitzjohns. Classic Andy Warhol, Roy Lichtenstein, and Max Wiedemann pieces can be admired here, as well as pieces by talented new artists. At number 48, you can enjoy works of art at BOSI Contemporary. The artistic, atmospheric Orchard Street, especially between Delancey Street and East Houston Street, draws a lot of visitors. On Sunday there is a street market.

Accessibility

 Delancey Street

 Essex Street

20

The New Museum

235 BOWERY, LOWER EAST SIDE

This modern museum has been recreated by Marcia Tucker of the Whitney Museum of American Art. She has noted that talented artists are not successful in getting their foot through the door of established museums. Her mission is to display contemporary art, no more than ten years old, to a large audience. And thus, the New Museum concept was launched! In 2001, two Japanese architects, Kazuyo Sejima and Ryue Nishizawa, were assigned to build the museum. The results are astonishing. On a relatively small property they stacked seven "shoeboxes," all of different sizes, to create large transparent rooms whereby the interaction between the artists and the public is optimized. The inside and outside worlds overlap. A lot of glass was used, which of course creates large surfaces. The only colors that have been used are in the bathrooms and the elevators. On the seventh floor you will find an enormous rooftop terrace with a wide view over New York, and the crooked streets in the Bowery area. That image is reflected in the museum's building plans. The New Museum offers a fascinating spectacle of light and space. Modern art forms such as social media art are displayed next to freestanding sculptures. A political dialogue is encouraged with its audience. In 2012 there was a large exhibition called The Ungovernables, displaying the works of about forty artists. Director Massimiliano Gioni attracts a lot of young artists from all over the world. In 2013 he was the director of the Venetian Biennale. The New Museum also works with the Van Abbemuseum in Eindhoven in the Netherlands.

Accessibility

Broadway - Lafayette Street

21

Dolce Vita

255 ELIZABETH STREET, NOLITA

Those who enjoy boutique shopping cannot miss this attractive shopping street in the north of Little Italy. In the eighties, many of the Italian Americans left and subsequently the yuppies took over the street. The prices of the houses increased considerably at this time. These days, the street is flourishing with galleries, fashion-, and interior-design joints. You will usually need to pack a nice, filled wallet to bring to this street, but that doesn't apply to Dolce Vita, which opened its doors in 2012. You would often find Dolce Vita shoes in the luxury department of the warehouses in all of America, but here the classically designed interior draws you in with its chandelier and antique cupboard that displays the whole collection—colorful and daring, with good quality and a lot of variation such as pumps, flats, and boots. Especially sexy high heels in all sorts of colors and motifs are very popular.

Because of their relatively low prices, their customers can also look in the casual section for comfortable clothing. Jewelry is also sold here. Dolce Vita is known to attract lots of young people.

dolce vita

Accessibility

Broadway - Lafayette Street

22

Tacombi at Fonda Mexican Restaurant

267 ELIZABETH STREET, NOLITA

Want to feel like you're in the lively Mexican square at the Playa del Carmen beach while in Manhattan? Then it's time to visit the trendy, fashion-forward Nolita garage. Authentic Mexican meals (at reasonable prices) are served out of an old Volkswagen van. Ordering with money tokens and serving food on special plates is definitely original. Their guacamole and chips are delicious, not to mention the crispy fish taco. Deliciously sweet drinks such as watermelon soda and sangria, as well as some remarkable beers, are also served here. The setup is quite simple. There is an easy atmosphere in this "village square." It is loud, and plants grown in large pots only add to the tropical experience. The staff are friendly and proud. "They might even be the best tacos north of the Rio Grande," one of the waitresses told us. Before you make an order, you can taste-test anything. You can even have breakfast here. Fresh tacos with eggs can be ordered à la carte.

Accessibility

B **D** **F** **M**

Broadway - Lafayette Street

23

Mariebelle

484 BROOME STREET, SOHO

Mariebelle sells the most extraordinary chocolate creations amid a romantic décor. It makes one think of a nineteenth-century café in Paris or Buenos Aires. Shop windows are filled with luxurious chocolate bonbons made of pure cocoa, but also chocolates filled with all sorts of fruit. High ceilings, opulent chandeliers, and classic china are only a few of the trademarks of this intimate facility. You can sip delicious hot chocolate at the cocoa bar. There is a large variety of chocolate delicacies, from pure chocolate chunks to the Aztec hot chocolate that is made of 72 percent pure Colombian cocoa and has a cinnamon aftertaste. The writing on the walls explains that chocolate is a blessing for our body and spirits. Classical music is played in the background. You can also lunch here. Mariebelle has its own chocolate factory in Greenpoint, Brooklyn (67 Guernsey Street).

Accessibility

 Spring Street

24

Dominique Ansel "Cronut" Bakery

189 SPRING STREET, SOHO

DOMINIQUE ANSEL BAKERY

189 spring street, new york, ny 10012
212.219.2773 ᴛᴇʟ | 917.591.2330 ꜰᴀх
www.dominiqueansel.com

The year of the cronut, a cross between a croissant and a donut, was 2013. The cronut is the crispy result of an amazing three-day baking process, created by Dominique Ansel. In May 2013 he started by selling these delicacies in his bakery. Since then there has been an impressive line of people lined from the front door to the street around the corner. They are five dollars per specimen, and limited to two per person. A black market has emerged amongst his customers. The smart ones offer to stand in line and buy these sweet treats for up to $40. There was even a man who offered himself up sexually, asking for a cronut in return. As the hype continued, Dominque tweeted his surprise when a woman burst into tears after standing in the line and hearing that they had sold out of cronuts. The cronut had obviously been a great hit. But, the bakery does offer other delicious treats. Dominique was once a dessert chef at the famous restaurant Daniel in New York. The bread is also delicious. Dominique remembered the incredible smell of fresh bread at his childhood bakery. This is what he meant the bakery in Soho to be like. Every thirty minutes, the loaves must be baked fresh. You can watch it yourself from their open kitchen. If you have to step away from the bakery scent, you can dine in the garden. The creative menu is constantly changing, though you can always order from two soups, five sandwiches, and three salads. The big news here is definitely "Down with the cupcakes, long live the cronut!"

Accessibility

Ⓐ Ⓒ Ⓔ

Spring Street

25

New York City
Fire Museum

278 SPRING STREET, SOHO

An original firefighting station in a beautiful Beaux Arts building. It is no wonder that this little museum, filled with firefighting artifacts, is admired by New Yorkers and tourists alike. The history of the firefighters is presented from the times of New Amsterdam up until the present. You will see how firefighters used to put out fires with buckets of water. In the nineteenth century, they used a horse and cart. The horses were often anxious about the roaring fires and were thus accompanied by dalmatians, who calmed the horses down. Even when the firefighters dove into the ocean of fires, the dalmatians would accompany them. Amid the antique objects and vehicles are present-day firefighters who are also guides of this museum. They love to tell their stories to visitors. This is clearly a museum with a soul. Previously, neighborhoods were filled with wooden houses, and there was a constant worry about fire danger. When something went wrong, the whole neighborhood woke up. The then-volunteer firefighters would serve their dangerous duty and were praised by their communities. The firefighting community was also meaningful in the political sense, as you will learn at the museum. This museum also has an impressive monument in honor of the 343 firefighters whose lives were taken during the attacks of 9/11. Visiting the collection will take about two hours, and is very suitable for children. In the gift shop children can buy a firefighter's suit, and of course a plush dalmatian.

Accessibility

Spring Street

26

Hamilton Fish Park

128 PITT STREET, LOWER EAST SIDE

New York had become the most densely populated city in the world by the end of the nineteenth century. Many poor immigrants streamed into this part of New York. Newspapers from this time note that immigrants slept on chairs and tables, in the overflowing apartment blocks. One of the narrow streets became known as Bone Alley because of its high death toll. The year 1900 brought a welcome expansion: a grand park with a bathhouse built in a luxurious Beaux Arts style. Beautiful terraces, walkways, and fountains around it gave the park an aristocratic feel. The Petit Palais in Paris was its greatest influence. The poor could also rest here. However, the visitors often trampled over the nature strips, and thus they had to be covered by cement.

In the middle of the Great Crisis of the thirties, during President Roosevelt's candidacy, many places were transformed to become public areas. Open-air swimming pools were placed in the park, even one of Olympic proportions. In the summer of that year, eleven pools opened in the city. Hamilton Fish Pool was mainly created so that people would no longer swim in the polluted East River. Free swimming still encourages people to visit the pools to this day to fight the heat of New York summers; it has become a family-favorite place. In the park you can still admire the Beaux Arts palace.

Accessibility

 Delancey Street

 Essex Street

27

Katz's Deli

**205 EAST HOUSTON STREET,
LOWER EAST SIDE**

There are still classic Jewish delis in New York. The most original deli can be found in the Lower East Side, a neighborhood in which apartments and hotels are constantly being built because of the number of tourists who want to visit this authentic part of New York. Katz's follows the trends because here you can buy their bestseller, the Reuben sandwich: a sandwich with pastrami, cabbage, and melted cheese. This combination of meat and cheese could previously never have been sold in a Jewish deli. Another recent addition to this 125-year-old, atmospheric joint is their recent twenty-four-hour service on weekends. This helps to draw the younger crowds on their nights out on the town. Katz's has always been a safe haven in this rough immigrant and working-class neighborhood, which had a lively drug scene during the eighties. Many things at Katz's have stayed the same. The same tables, chairs, and signs. The receipt system is legendary and leads a patron from counter to counter. Their famous sign from World War II still hangs on the wall: "Send a salami to your boy in the army." This is also a line from a well-known war song. These days Katz's delivers surprise packages to the soldiers in foreign countries such as Iraq. Pastrami originates from Romania as cured meat, brought to New York by immigrants. A famous scene from the film *When Harry Met Sally*, in which Sally simulates an orgasm after eating a Katz's sandwich, was acted out in this store. The table at which they sat still stands in the same spot and is photographed by its many patrons. The recipe of the sandwiches that are piled with meat is top secret. An average of forty-four thousand pounds of meat is used per week, half of which is pastrami, and a quarter of which is corned beef. Three to four thousand hot dogs and twelve thousand pickles are also sold per week.

Accessibility

 Lower East Side - 2nd Avenue

28

John Derian

6 EAST 2ND STREET, BETWEEN 2ND AVENUE/BOWERY, EAST VILLAGE

I n 1989 John Derian created a store in which he could experiment with decoupage, the art of decorating an object. Soon it seemed he had great talent. He collected nineteenth-century paper prints of beautiful still lifes, and worked them into glass objects to place in one's home. His birds, fruit, and flowers match traditional as well as modern interiors. This tucked-away shopping paradise is filled with artistic home wares from his own studio but also with china and fabrics from great designers.

There is also an elaborate collection of candles whose scents can transport you to Cape Cod, Delhi, and Jerusalem. This place in the trendy East Village exudes a Parisian aesthetic. Derian has visited many flea markets, secondhand stores, and antique stores in Clignancourt where they display its beautiful findings. Their leather poofs, lamps from Morocco, and kilts from Pakistan are also popular. Derian has a large variety of admirers. You will never be alone in this store. A blogger wrote: "From the moment you step inside, you will feel a sense of pure joy because of all of the luxurious, beautiful, colorful, and happy home items . . . I wish this store was my home." Do you recognize John Derian? Pretty much every magazine in the world that writes about lifestyle and interiors has also written about "the master of paper, glass, and glue," from *Vogue* to *Vanity Fair*. The *Wall Street Journal* calls Derian "something of a global sensation."

Accessibility

(4) (6) (D) (F)

Broadway -
Lafayette Street/Bleecker Street

29

Curve

57 BOND STREET, NOHO, EAST VILLAGE

evena Borissova is an absolute fashion sensation. As a child she emigrated from Bulgaria to the United States. She didn't finish high school, but had part-time jobs in several fashion stores. Nevena had a special sense for fashion and successfully opened up her own boutique in Los Angeles at the age of twenty-two. Now she has opened five, the largest and most recent one being on Bond Street: luxurious and super trendy. Stars such as Céline Dion and Alicia Keys buy their clothes at Curve. The *New York Times* called her "a whirlwind that cannot be stopped with a nose for everything that's new." She sells brands such as Isabel Marant, Fausto Puglisi, and Viktor & Rolf. Shoes, bags, and jewelry are also sold in this large boutique with high ceilings that does the collection justice. Borissova also has her own black-and-white fashion line in the store: A. O. T. C., or in other words, Ahead of the Curve. The line Curve HOMME also represents men's clothing.

Accessibility

Broadway -
Lafayette Street/Bleecker Street

30

A POP UP SET

Arch... ...els

Egyptian Pharohs
Hand-Painted Pieces

Pearl Harb...
America vs...

15" Red / Coral Marble
Pieces and Board
in Velvet Box

Chess Forum and Restaurant Cuba

219 AND 222 THOMPSON STREET, GREENWICH VILLAGE

An old Eastern carpet, a giant collection of chessboards in glass cases, and tables at the back where you can play. For those who enjoy anything to do with chess, this is the place to be. To play chess for an hour will cost you a few dollars. You're alone? Who will play with you? No problem, because every other minute someone from the neighborhood, or even just a tourist, will walk in. The sympathetic owner is the walking embodiment of the noble sport of chess. Once there was a serious chess war on Thompson Street. The many chess joints challenged each other in a matter of life-or-death games. Chess Forum has stayed intact, but now faces its challenges by competing against chess online. The owner says, "I tell mothers that their children should learn to play chess physically. They learn to lend a hand, create real contacts. Friendships are made here."

The best view of the Chess Forum is at night. The regulars from the neighborhood and all walks of life stroll in. The dimmed lights center on the boards. In the background, Mozart softly plays. The conversations range from Shakespeare and new music shows to the world's situations, now and of the future. And, of course, chess. That's where the name comes from. It is also the ideal place to buy a chessboard; they have a very unique collection.

Hungry for a snack? On the opposite side of the road is Cuba, one of the better Cuban restaurants that serves authentic dishes. This is as good an occasion as any to try a mojito. It's quite a small but very atmospheric joint, with regular live music acts, and sometimes even a Cuban cigar maker who rolls his cigars in a corner.

Accessibility

West 4th Street

Murray's Cheese Shop

254 BLEECKER STREET (BETWEEN 6TH AND 7TH AVENUES), WEST GREENWICH VILLAGE

hose who think the best cheese is only sold in The Netherlands will find themselves sorely mistaken in this cheese paradise. American and European cheeses are displayed in all shapes and sizes—soft, hard, or creamy. This atmospheric joint has been settled in Greenwich Village for seventy years. Generously, many taste-tests are offered to customers. They also provide a cheese class here, where you can learn to make mozzarella, the most popular cheese in New York. Aside from the traditional process of making cheese, there are also wine, beer, and liqueur tastings. The cheese tour takes you to the cheese cellars. There are even a few "cheese boot camps." Over the course of three days, you can learn everything there is to know about cheese, which will be proved with the certificate you'll receive at the end. Murray's also sells salads, salamis, and olives. Their grilled-cheese sandwich and the tuna melt are also very popular. The staff are real specialists and are very helpful. They are also artists when it comes to assembling a cheese platter. As they talk with you, they are completely focused on your personal taste buds so that you will slowly but surely become addicted to Murray's cheeses. Need an original greeting to send to the home front as a souvenir from New York? Fret not, as there is a large collection of cheese greeting cards. Want to stay a bit longer in the cheese world? For a real cheese meal, accompanied by the most delicious wines, make your way to Murray's Cheese Bar, just three doors down. Murray's slogans are "We know cheese" and "Say cheese and walk out smiling."

Accessibility

West 4th Street

Washington Square "Sixties" Mural

125 MACDOUGAL STREET, WEST GREENWICH VILLAGE

This street is sacred ground for admirers of the sixties. You'll find everything here: old music clubs, theaters, and coffee shops. Bob Dylan first set foot in the Village after arriving from Minnesota in January 1961. His first appearance was at 115 in Café Wha?. The Groove at number 127 is still open seven days a week and is the place to be for rhythm and blues funk music. One of the walls displays a remarkable mural painted with bright colors. Beneath the text "Keep the spirit of the sixties alive" are portraits of the Beatles, Jimi Hendrix, Albert Einstein, and Bob Dylan playing his guitar and harmonica. The creator of this mural is the popular Peruvian Rico Fonseca, who has lived in the Village for thirty years. The whole neighborhood breathes in the spirit of Bob Dylan and his peers from the sixties. Bob Dylan gathered his friends, and on a Sunday afternoon they went to the fountain in Washington Park to sing songs. During the nineteenth century, Washington Square was still on the outside of the city and was being used as a mass grave site for the poor. It even served as a gallows field. The oldest tree in Manhattan on which people were hanged, also known as the "Hanging Tree," is still there. Eventually, it became a park, and writers such as Ernest Hemingway moved into the neighborhood. Around the corner at 103 Washington Place is the atmospheric Washington Square boutique hotel where Hemingway lived for a little while, just as The Mamas & the Papas, Joan Baez, and Bob Dylan did. His room number was 305. The excellent hotel restaurant, North Square, caters jazz brunches on Sundays. Norah Jones used to serve here as a waitress. Even now, there are still many musicians at Washington Square Park. Don't be surprised if you hear the sounds of "Blowin' in the Wind" as Bob Dylan once allegedly sang it at the fountain.

Accessibility

West 4th Street

33

La Lanterna di Vittorio

129 MACDOUGAL STREET, WEST VILLAGE

his is one of the most romantic restaurants in New York.

 This old building was built by a former vice president of the United States, Aaron Burr. The great speaker and politician once dueled a competitor and set off a deadly shot. The greatest eye-catcher is the two-hundred-year-old canopied back garden, where large colorful lamps create an atmospheric scene. A fireplace is also stoked on colder days. This warm décor uses small tables to add to the intimate feel. The pizzas, the lasagna, and the delicious desserts are very popular. Other standouts on the menu include the bresaola meats, the panna cotta, and, of course, the variants of gelati.

 There is also an elaborate wine list. Within its own Bar Next Door, downstairs, there is a valued jazz club. Real jazz enthusiasts come here to discuss with musicians the values of jazz traditions as well as its new challenges. Prices at La Lanterna are very reasonable. The fresh mojitos, with mint from their own garden, attract many New York University students to the restaurant.

Accessibility

A C E D F

West 4th Street

34

Washington Square Arch

WASHINGTON SQUARE, GREENWICH VILLAGE

George Washington, America's first president, was inaugurated in New York. To celebrate this, one hundred years later, in 1889, a series of triumphant arches was built under which parades could be marched in celebration. The most beautiful was at Washington Square at the start of Fifth Avenue. This timely piece of art was built of wood and plaster. Well-off families that established themselves in the pillar houses at Washington Square opted for a permanent marble monument. Under the leadership of William Rhinelander Stewart, a sum of $150,000 was collected. In 1891 the time had come. George Washington's arch of victory, similar to the Arc de Triomphe, was a statement of the architectonic grandeur of the neighborhood. The Village was an oasis, but the city of the poor immigrant communities marched on. The cheap tenement buildings expanded from the Lower East Side and the East Village to the edge of Washington Square. Maybe there lies the secret of bohemian culture that is still so prominent in this area. The establishment of New York University also created a unique community of culture-loving mercenaries, down-and-outers, artists, and students.

Accessibility

West 4th Street

One of the rich art lovers who settled in the Village was Gertrude Vanderbilt Whitney. She took pity on young, rebellious artists such as John Sloan and Marcel Duchamp. This duo climbed the arch, armed with Chinese lanterns, red balloons, and canisters of tea on January 23, 1917. Their protest was to appeal to the Boston Tea Party. With this ludicrous action, they declared Washington Square as a free, sovereign republic, independent of uptown, where many museums were built, including the Metropolitan Museum that did not display any modern works of art. The surrounding areas of the arch have never lost that free spirit. Freedom and tolerance were preached through painters such as Hopper, Pollock, and De Kooning, by philosophers such as Kerouac and Ginsberg, and now by the gay movement in the Village. The spirit of the Village is still unbroken. The arch is a continuous symbol, with its designs of George Washington as a citizen and as a soldier as created by Calder and MacNeil. The arch as a whole was designed by Stanford White. Washington Square is a monument of artistic and social rebellion.

35

La Petite Coquette

51 UNIVERSITY PLACE, GREENWICH VILLAGE

Rebecca Apsan wrote a well-known lingerie handbook, and puts her knowledge to the test in her own lingerie store. The interior is romantic with a slight touch of naughtiness. The staff are very friendly and they have almost every size imaginable. From classic to super-trendy styles, their products are functional and tasteful, with a specialty in bras. Well-known brands such as Wendy Glez, Hanky Panky, and Andrés Sardá are sold here, but they also offer their own line of lingerie. You can even personalize your lingerie by putting the name of a loved one on it. Swimwear and panty hose are also sold here. This store is in competition with Victoria's Secret because of their personal customer service, expertise, and scale. This pearl in the Village is not cheap, but they do often have sales.

Those who wish to prepare something for their wedding or Valentine's Day should take the opportunity to visit La Petite Coquette. The slogan here is "There is 'coquette' in every customer." This boutique with its Parisian touch delivered its lingerie to the actors on *Sex and the City*. Marlies Dekkers was sold here first.

Accessibility

N **R**

8th Street - New York University

36

C. O. Bigelow "America's Oldest Pharmacy"

414 6TH AVENUE, GREENWICH VILLAGE

Want to visit the times of "Mom and Dad" in the heart of New York? Then it's time to take the sentimental journey to the pharmacy that was already this neighborhood's pharmacy in 1838. Thomas Edison once came here to get his finger treated, and Eleanor Roosevelt was a regular customer. In this *shop* you will find the most remarkable toothpastes, lip balms, and hotel soaps, but also the famous lemon body crème that has been sold here since 1870. The store originates from the time when the pharmacist had a remedy for every trouble. This was a warm place that the neighbors could come into for a chat. The cats who visited throughout the years became celebrities. They were fed by patrons, who brought along their own treats. The cats became really fat; one even weighed up to forty pounds. Alas, the soda fountain has since disappeared, though you can still admire the gas lanterns and old counters. This father-son business is named after its previous owner.

Accessibility

Ⓐ Ⓒ Ⓔ Ⓓ Ⓕ

West 4th Street

37

Gay Liberation Monument

CHRISTOPHER PARK, 53 CHRISTOPHER STREET, WEST VILLAGE

You are now entering a tiny public garden that is sacred ground in the gay community. The park is across from the famous Stonewall Inn. After regular police raids started at this tavern and bar in 1969, the first large gay protest presented itself. The first Gay and Lesbian Pride Parade was organized here in 1970. In his second inauguration in 2013, President Obama made a connection between this "Stonewall moment" and the black civil rights movement. In 1979, George Segal accepted the assignment to design a liberation monument, after many sculptors had declined. The only demand of the businessman and assigner of the project, Peter Putman, was that the monument should portray love and care. "It should show the affection that people often identify with gay people . . . and it has to represent men as well as women." Segal is famous for his bronze sculptures of ordinary people, such as unemployed people from the thirties waiting at a food counter at the Franklin Roosevelt Monument in Washington. In Christopher Park we can see two men and two women talking to each other as they touch each other. The monument attracts extra attention, as it is painted white. After all sorts of protests, the monument was finally revealed on June 22, 1992. At 61 Christopher Street is Duplex, a famous piano and cabaret bar owned by the same people as the Stonewall Inn.

Accessibility

Christopher Street - Sheridan Square

38

55 Bar

55 CHRISTOPHER STREET, WEST VILLAGE

55 BAR
Live Jazz & Blues Every Night!
MUSIC COVER CHARGE **$12**
55 Christopher St.
Tel: 212-929-9883
Check www.55bar.com for schedule and band info!

The 55 Bar is an underground jazz and blues palace across from the gay monument in the heart of the Village. It is also of walking distance from Marie's Crisis and Arthur's Tavern. This is the place to be for jazz and blues. During the twenties, the 55 Bar was a speakeasy. There are two shows every night. This narrow room is a sympathetic business. The concoctions are reasonably priced, though there is a two-drink minimum. Often there is a humble entrance fee for the second, later show. The bar staff understand their area of expertise as well as the music that is played there. Remarkable young talent is also given a chance to play here as well as some of the world's best jazz guitarists such as Mike Stern, a regular on the stage. For a number of years he played with Blood, Sweat & Tears and was part of the Miles Davis Comeback Band. He now plays with his own band. Blues singer Sweet Georgia Brown, not to be confused with the song of the same title, is a female singer who performed at 55 Bar

and Arthur's Tavern. "Dark, cozy, sexy, and hot music," as a critic recently noted. To illustrate the history: the older patrons of the bar have been visiting since the fifties and distinctly remember the boiled egg that used to cook in the water. To serve alcohol, one also had to serve food.

Accessibility

1 **2**

Christopher Street - Sheridan Square

39

Marie's Crisis Piano Bar and Arthur's Tavern

57 AND 59 GROVE STREET, 7TH AVENUE, WEST VILLAGE

Every evening until deep in the night, passersby can hear the show tunes from *West Side Story*, *Mary Poppins*, and *Chicago*. This dark basement bar is the place to be for those who want to taste the atmosphere of the old Village. Every night up-and-coming Broadway stars gather around the piano to passionately sing these songs. You're allowed to sing along, but that's up to you. Marie's Crisis is somewhat of a magical place—a simple, narrow room where mysterious stories are told. In 1809 the revolutionary thinker Thomas Paine, who wrote *The Crisis Papers*, died here. Paine passionately wrote about freedom. "These are the times that try men's souls" was one of his famous expressions. He stood up to the British monarchical dominion.

The previous owner Marie Du Mont named part of the building after the famous writer and thinker. During the mid-nineteenth century it was a brothel; during the thirties amid Prohibition it was a speakeasy and a boys' bar. Behind the bar there is a mirror that nobody seems to know the history of, which displays images of the French and American Revolutions. The older patrons tell stories of spirits that haunt the premises. Marie's Crisis is an informal bar where everyone is welcome. On weekends it is often very busy. Dexter is our favorite pianist, especially when he plays "All That Jazz." At number 57 is Arthur's Tavern, a New York record, jazz, and blues bar that has been there for over seventy-five years. Entry here is still free. Celebrities such as Charlie Parker and Roy Hargrove performed here. In this "Home of the Bird" there is a remarkable and enormous bar. Christmas lights shine here throughout the whole year, and there is often a chance to enjoy "Sweet Georgia Brown."

Accessibility

Christopher Street - Sheridan Square

40

Garden of
St. Luke in the Fields

478 HUDSON STREET, WEST VILLAGE

This English-landscape garden lies between houses that, according to the landscape commission of New York, are the oldest and most beautiful in the Village. Those who are tired after walking through these beautiful streets cannot imagine a more perfect place to rest than here. Between the entrance on Hudson Street and the worn brick wall of the St. Luke church is a green and flowery oasis. In the center stands a large tree with white flowers. Around this area is a grass field where, weather pending, you will find many people resting. Four paths lead along the flower beds of mostly roses in all sorts of colors. There are many remarkable butterfly species here too. The church is from 1821. The first planting in 1842 consisted of a twig from the famous Glastonbury thornbush from England, the sacred plant that blossoms twice a year. The garden has a spiritual aspect to it. Whoever enters is encouraged to turn off their cell phone and to speak softly. Many meditate on the benches in the corners of the garden. The Episcopal church "for everybody" is very popular in the neighborhood that suffered fiercely from the AIDS epidemic. There is a lot of charity work here. The church is always strongly represented in the gay parades and also has female ministers.

Accessibility

Christopher Street - Sheridan Square

41

Strand Bookstore

828 BROADWAY, CORNER OF 12TH STREET, EAST VILLAGE

WHERE BOOKS ARE LOVED
STRAND
NEW YORK CITY ★ EST. 1927

Nosing around in a "book lovers' paradise"! Inside and out, in all nooks and crannies, there are about 2.5 million books on display. Books that are old and new, and often marked down. In 1927 Strand began as a small shop founded by Benjamin Bass. He borrowed $300, placed a cigar case down, and set out to fill the place with his own book collection. On "Book Row" there used to be forty bookstores. The Strand survived them all. One of the success factors is the expert staff who will find your book no matter what. There is a special collection of remarkable books that either are unique first-print editions or are signed by the author. There is also a remarkable collection of art books on the first floor. If you were to line up all of the books, they would cover about eighteen miles. Columnist George Will once wrote in the fifties that if New York ever went under, the only thing that should remain is the Strand mile. Strolling through the store is a real tradition for many New Yorkers. Don't expect any luxurious coffee bars or lunchrooms here. Those can easily be found on the same street where you can admire your new purchases.

Accessibility

(4) (5) (6)

14th Street - Union Square

42

Greenmarket
Union Square

EAST 17TH STREET – BROADWAY, FLATIRON DISTRICT

With statues of George Washington, Abraham Lincoln, and Mahatma Gandhi, Union Square from 1839 is a political square. This is where the first Labor Day parade took place. There were regular protests from socialists and workers on strike, and large memorials are held such as the one on 9/11. The word union does not relate to the workers union but rather to the union between Broadway and the then Bowery Road, now 4th Avenue. In 1970, Earth Day was founded here. That environmentally conscious tradition is still a characteristic of the atmospheric farmers market held here throughout the entire year on Mondays, Wednesdays, Fridays, and Saturdays from 8:00 a.m. to 6:00 p.m. It started in 1976 with just a few stalls; now there are approximately 150 sellers of super-fresh and often cheap natural produce. Aside from the tourists, many New Yorkers visit here for the healthy and organic foods. Many master chefs from renowned restaurants buy their fresh produce here. It is thanks to the "Greenmarket movement" that many farmers could hold their head above the water. There is a large variety of food and drink, from pure honey to fresh apple cider. Students are taught in the open-air setting about healthy eating; leftover foods are donated to the needy. At the end of November is the start of the popular Christmas market, where you can buy lots of traditional presents. You can lunch, dine, or sit at the bar in the Union Square Café on 21st and 16th Streets for very reasonable prices. Of course, all their ingredients come from Greenmarket.

Accessibility

14th Street - Union Square

43

High Line

MANY ENTRANCES, THE OLDEST ON GANSEVOORT STREET, CHELSEA

During the mid-nineteenth century New York gave permission for railroads to be laid down, all the way to South Manhattan. Special "West Side Cowboys" were assigned as safety patrols; they waved their flags in front of oncoming trains. The local commission gave in to the safety concerns of local citizens. At the start of the thirties an overhead, aboveground railway was built stretching thirteen miles. The trains that brought fuel and food to the city drove up until the factory buildings, like the Nabisco cookie factory, now known as the Chelsea Market. Because of the increase in international road traffic, the last stocked train rode over these rails in 1980 carrying frozen turkeys. Soon, remarkable wild grasses and wildflowers started to blossom here. It's thanks to the neighborhood's Peter Obletz and his compatriots that the park has received so much attention since then. The High Line was now to resemble the Promenade Plantée in Paris. Two miles have been open to the public and provide a beautiful panoramic scene. There are lots of benches and reclining chairs. A large part of the park is still made up of natural growth. There are remarkable works of art such as the glass "The River That Flows Both Ways" by Spencer Finch, which has increased the impact of the nearby Hudson River. The stretched-out park has many buildings of which the Standard Hotel presents the true renaissance of the neighborhood. The High Line has many entrances. The one on Gansevoort Street leads to the oldest part. The Dutchman Piet Oudolf is one of the designers of High Line Park, and a company from Amsterdam worked on the roof growth and the watering systems.

Accessibility

A C E

23rd Street

44

Chelsea Market

75 9TH AVENUE, BETWEEN 15TH AND 16TH STREETS

At the end of the nineteenth century, a cookie factory was inside this impressive building. It was the birthplace of the famous, round, chocolate cookie with white cream filling. The beautiful name "Oreo" could relate to its original gold (*or* in French) packaging. The cookie factory, since then, has closed. Now you can take a stroll amid what is left of the post-industrial era along stalls, fresh markets, and restaurants. If you look for it, you might still be able to see the old mosaic letters "NBC," which stood for the National Biscuit Company. Chelsea Market is a food paradise that will serve you things such as fresh lobster and sushi, freshly prepared by the unique Lobster Place. Or you can enjoy Japanese food at Masaharu Morimoto, as the "iron chef" from the cooking show *Food Network* exercises his trade in this building. The most delicious and most remarkable pastas, cheeses, and other delicacies spread their scents across the market. Our taste tip is the Caramel Baby at the Fat Witch Factory: a treat with a crispy outer layer and a soft, decadent chocolate filling. For those who like white chocolate there is also the Snow White Brownie. There is definitely a fan club of sorts dedicated to these "witch brownies."

During happy hour, after five, there are extra-special sales offers. It would be smart to visit this place during the week, as it can be very busy on weekends.

Accessibility

14th Street

45

SPICE MARKET

CULINARYCONCEPTS.COM

Meatpacking District

BETWEEN GANSEVOORT STREET, THE HIGH LINE, AND 14TH STREET

Around the year 1900, there were about 250 meat businesses here. These days, it is a trendy boutique and restaurant area. The bistro Pastis, currently under renovation, will remind you of Paris in the thirties. The Niçoise salad cannot be beaten. The remarkable Spice Market of Jean-Georges Vongerichten will serve you dishes from Southeast Asia in a warm, attractive ambience. Our favorites include the herbed Vietnamese chicken and the grilled steak with coriander, sesame, and garlic. The ginger margarita cocktail is also delicious. STK, "Steak," is also hot and trendy. The steaks are in all shapes and sizes. The Porterhouse is especially loved by its patrons, but there are many more to choose from. The tuna starter, as well as many other fish dishes, is amazing. You should also try the parmesan and truffle fries. STK is half restaurant, half lounge, and on top of that it also has a great roof terrace with a beautiful view of the High Line. The interior has many rounded intimate seating areas with white leather furnishings. It gives the restaurant a chic feel, which acts as a magnet to the young and the old as well as those who come for either business or pleasure. Buddakan is the fourth absolute winner. This dark, cathedral-like restaurant with romantic candlelight is a superb mix of Asian, French, and American cuisines. Also popular for an after-dinner drink are the rooftop bars Le Bain, The Standard hotel, and the bar at the Gansevoort Hotel.

© Todd Eberle

Accessibility

Ⓐ Ⓒ Ⓔ

14th Street

46

David Zwirner Gallery

WEST 525 19TH STREET, CHELSEA

n Chelsea, there have been roughly four hundred art galleries since the nineties. One of the most famous is David Zwirner's gallery. Zwirner is the son of a German art dealer who emigrated to America and made a fortune with his art collection. In his large art gallery in Chelsea, you will often find minimalistic art, such as the plain blocks by Donald Judd, and the colored planks by John McCracken, but also photography by Thomas Ruff. Luc Tuymans is one of the most famous artists that has been represented by Zwirner. De Vlaming paints discomforting, figurative pieces on cloth. For instance, his work regarding the Holocaust: one of the objects in the painting is a lampshade made of human parts of those from the concentration camp in Buchenwald. He often uses photographic techniques. Zwirner also gives unknown artists a chance. Those emerging artists who are represented in Zwirner's gallery are ensured a bright future. *The Guardian*, *Forbes Magazine*, and many other media outlets place David Zwirner in the top of New York's galleries. There is also a David Zwirner gallery in London.

Accessibility

23rd Street

47

THEODORE ROOSEVELT
WAS BORN HERE
OCTOBER 27, 1858.
BIRTHPLACE REPRODUCED
BY THE
THEODORE ROOSEVELT MEMORIAL ASSOCIATION
JANUARY 6, 1921.

28

President Theodore Roosevelt's Birthplace

28 EAST 20TH STREET, FLATIRON DISTRICT

america's most colorful president (1901–1909) was born on October 27, 1858, in this house. The original brownstone house was torn down in 1916, but was later rebuilt as a replica including some original Roosevelt artifacts. The widow of the president, as well as his two sisters, donated a lot of furniture to the free Roosevelt museum. The guide thoroughly explains the turbulent life of the young Roosevelt, who, as a child, suffered from asthma and was thus secluded to the house. This didn't take away from his great plans as he set up a "national natural history museum" in the house and displayed a large quantity of stuffed animals from the area. In the yard he practiced for hours on end boxing his punching bag to conquer his weak state of health. You can admire Roosevelt here as a hunter, soldier, and politician. The many hunting artifacts as well as the famous "Rough Rider" uniform are proof of his passions. During the invasion on Cuba to free our "brown brothers" from the colonial yoke, he stormed out in front of the troops, without armor, over a hill, and considered it an honor to kill a Spanish soldier. One remarkable object is the shirt with a bullet hole in it. In 1912 on his journey to Milwaukee, the president was shot. Against the advice of his doctors, Roosevelt decided to give his speech. The fifty sheets of paper placed in his pocket had stopped the bullet. Roosevelt spoke the historical words: "It takes more than that to kill a Bull Moose" (Bull Moose became his nickname). Roosevelt spoke for more than an hour as his shirt slowly turned red. Recently, some six hundred objects were taken from the house and have been replaced by replicas. Roosevelt lived in this neo-gothic house until he was fourteen years old.

THEODORE ROOSEVELT
WAS BORN HERE
OCTOBER 27, 1858
BIRTHPLACE REPRODUCED
BY THE
WOMAN'S ROOSEVELT MEMORIAL ASSOCIATION
JANUARY 6, 1921

Accessibility

 23rd Street

48

Gramercy Park

BETWEEN 3RD AVENUE, PARK AVENUE SOUTH,
EAST 18TH STREET, AND EAST 22ND STREET

GRAMERCY PARK HISTORIC DISTRICT

The Gramercy Park Historic District provides an early example of creative town planning. The area was developed in 1831 by Samuel B. Ruggles who laid out lots around New York City's only surviving private park. Buyers of the lots became joint owners of the park and each received a key to the gate. Original townhouses in Greek Revival, Italianate, Gothic Revival and Victorian Gothic styles still line the south and west sides of the square. The Friends Meeting House of the 1850's and one of the city's earliest apartment houses, built in 1883, are at the southeast corner. Plaque provided by the Trustees of Gramercy Park 1981

Gramercy Park is the only private park of Manhattan. In 1844 the park was "locked up." The coveted 383 keys are in the hands of the owners of beautiful townhouses and brownstones that surround the park. Others are not allowed to hold the keys. An exception has been made for the Gramercy Park Hotel that holds twelve keys for its guests. Whoever uses the keys is guided by a staff member through the gate and can take up to five guests with them. In the past, people have tried to copy the keys by going as far as Europe, but these days it is almost impossible. Every year a new, ingenious lock is created for all four entry gates, and the new keys are stored like museum pieces. If you lose the key, the fine is over $1,000. The park still attracts a lot of visitors, but all they can do is sit on a bench and look in, or jog around the park. In the green oasis are four flower beds next to a statue of neighbor Edwin Booth, a famous Shakespearian actor and brother of President Lincoln's assassin. On Christmas Eve, the park opens to the public and carols are sung beneath the giant Christmas tree. The nearby Gramercy Park Hotel is worth a visit. The Jade and Rose Bars are chic and hip at the same time. It also displays works of art from Andy Warhol. This is a cute, exclusive place for a cocktail or a martini, for example. There is also a nice roof terrace that you can visit for lunch for up to three hours. The word Gramercy is from the Dutch *krom moerasje*.

Accessibility

4 **6** 23rd Street

49

UCB Theater

307 WEST 26TH STREET, CHELSEA

The letters UCB stand for the Upright Citizens Brigade. If you wish to experience comedy as well as conference of a high level, at a small price, then UCB is the perfect choice for you. The doors of this old factory comedy club opened in 2003. Number of seats: 150. Don't expect any cushions. UCB is very popular amongst New Yorkers with its twenty-five unique shows per week. There can be up to four shows per night. One of the local favorites is Amy Poehler, known from her performances on *Saturday Night Live* and Comedy Central—Poehler brought the house down with her Hillary Clinton impression. You are not obliged to buy a drink at this one! UCB is also in Los Angeles and trains young people for a career in film, theater, and television. The UCB employees worked for Jon Stewart's *The Daily Show* and David Letterman's *The Late Show*. Robin Williams used to perform, and it's known that Conan O'Brien might show up, but you would have to pay $5 to $10 to see that! Only cash is accepted, and you can reserve seats via their website. Take care to show up half an hour early to stand in line.

Accessibility

23rd Street

50

Koreatown

WEST 32ND STREET, MIDTOWN

Spontaneously, Koreatown, also known as Korea Way, and K-town, emerged between 5th and 6th Avenues. It started in the eighties when a Korean bookstore and one restaurant opened their doors. Now, the whole block between Fifth Avenue and Broadway is filled with Korean businesses. In Korea, the businesses revolve around one thing: location, location, location. If a store or eatery draws a lot of attention somewhere, entrepreneurs will want to get as close to that success as possible, sometimes literally on top of the successful business. In this way, many businesses are stacked on top of each other. The same development happened in Koreatown, New York. It is close to Macy's, the Empire State Building, and Penn Station. In this region of New York live some two hundred thousand Korean citizens. Usually as night falls, and on the weekends, Koreatown draws its customers in. Many neon signs light the streets just as in Seoul, and you can eat typical Korean dishes such as Korean sushi, fried chicken, tofu dishes, and all sorts of sweet treats.

For many Koreans, a visit here becomes a sentimental journey. One of the better restaurants is called Miss Korea. Other excellent restaurants are Poncha 32, Arang, and BCD Tofu House (praised by the *New York Times*). The Paris Baguette Bakery is a popular chain in Koreatown. This tasteful place is great for getting a taste of the Korean atmosphere. There are also many karaoke bars in Koreatown.

Accessibility

N **R** 28th Street

51

Annex Hell's Kitchen
Flea Market

WEST 39TH STREET, BETWEEN 9TH AND 10TH AVENUES, MIDTOWN WEST

A flea market as flea markets should be, and with lots of local sellers. Colorful people! Atmospheric. The market is "hidden" between the Lincoln Tunnel and the large bus station of New York, the Port Authority. It is walking distance from Times Square, in the heart of the city. The market isn't too big; it has 170 stalls. Here you can find jewelry, secondhand clothing of many top market brands, and a lot of American knickknacks. The Amish products are very popular. In the past few years the well-known previously Annex antique market from Chelsea has also been added to it. This combined flea market is the place to be for a rustic waffle iron, an aged typewriter, and that old Coca-Cola bottle. The market is open every Saturday and Sunday of the year from 9:00 a.m. until 6:00 p.m., and with enough space to walk around. The best buys are often displayed during the morning. Can't get enough of it? A shuttle bus will bring you to the Antiques Garage, a smaller market about twenty blocks farther up in Chelsea: two filled, decorated hallways for the bargain hunters.

Accessibility

(A) (C) (E)

42nd Street -
Port Authority Bus Terminal

52

Rose Main Reading Room

476 FIFTH AVENUE - 42ND STREET, MIDTOWN

New York had many libraries, even during the nineteenth century, and around the millennium change is when, with the help of philanthropists, a central library of majestic proportions was founded. In 1911 this Beaux Arts–style book temple was opened. Those who enter pass two marble lions with the nicknames Patience and Fortitude. Mayor La Guardia created these named in the crisis of the thirties because he felt that every New Yorker of the time needed to see this to survive. Via the bronze doors you will enter Astor Hall, named after the first American multimillionaire. In this giant library are the Gutenberg Bible, Shakespeare's works, and a handwritten Declaration of Independence from Thomas Jefferson. There are tours every day. You mustn't forget to visit the Rose Main Reading Room on the third floor. It stretches over two blocks of streets. Take a seat at one of the many oak tables: it offers you a special experience in this busy-world city, under the high, painted ceilings and the beautiful chandeliers. There is a serene sense of rest here. Literary giants such as Norman Mailer, Elizabeth Bishop, and Alfred Kazin were regular visitors. Dutch architect Francine Houben of Mecanoo is leading the renovation of the library.

In his memoirs, Kazin wrote about his reading experiences:

"There was something about the light falling through the great tall windows, the sun burning smooth the tops of the golden tables as if they had been freshly painted—that made me restless with the need to grab up every book, press into every single mind right there on the open shelves."

Accessibility

 Fifth Avenue - Bryant Park

53

Whispering Gallery and Oyster Bar

GRAND CENTRAL TERMINAL, 89 EAST 42ND STREET, MIDTOWN EAST

Planning a unique proposal? Grand Central is the place to be. It is the largest train station in the world and is located on Vanderbilt Avenue, between Madison Avenue and Lexington Avenue. New Yorkers are in love with this station. There are forty-four platforms and sixty-seven railways. In the food court is the Whispering Gallery. The acoustics are unique to this place due to the special construction of the bows. Someone who whispers in a certain corner can be heard loud and clear by their loved one on the other side. This free attraction draws many visitors. It has been said to be jazz legend Charles Mingus's favorite stage. Grand Central opened in 1871. It is a beautiful Jugendstil work of art. The clock at the entrance is made up of the largest amount of Tiffany glass in the world. The station is a treasure chamber of stories. President Roosevelt arrived regularly at a secret platform. From here, a lift would secretly deliver him to the Waldorf Astoria. Unfortunately this route has now been closed to the general public. But, there is still plenty to see. Amid the painted starry sky of the terminal you can see a dark circle. In 1957, in fear of a Russian rocket attack, an American "Redstone" rocket was placed in the hall. The hole in the ceiling was created to anchor a wire to stabilize the rocket. If you wish to make a culinary visit, then we recommend visiting the Grand Central Oyster Bar. This famous establishment is across from the Whispering Gallery. The fictional James Bond once dined here. It is often very busy, as people stop in while waiting for their train. You can choose from various types of oysters and wines. The Manhattan clam chowder soup is also a popular dish.

Accessibility

4 **5** **5**

Grand Central - 42nd Street

54

The Knotted Gun
United Nations

UNITED NATIONS VISITORS PLAZA, 1ST AVENUE, EAST SIDE

n and around the UN building (1952) are many works of art that communicate a peaceful message. These are gifts from various countries. Japan has donated a Peace Bell. Remarkable is the gift from Luxembourg made by the Swedish Carl Fredrik Reuterswärd. He was friends with John Lennon. After his death, Yoko Ono asked Reuterswärd to design a monument in honor of John that shows a peaceful world without violence. She directed him to the lyrics of "Imagine"

"You may say that I'm a dreamer
But I'm not the only one
I hope someday you will join us
And the world will live as one"

The knotted bronze sculpture used to stand at Strawberry Fields, but in 1988 was placed at the UN headquarters building. During its acceptance ceremony, Secretary-General Kofi Annan said the following:

"The sculpture, Nonviolence, has not only endowed the United Nations with a work of art to cherish; it has enriched the consciousness of humanity with a powerful symbol that encapsulates, in a few simple curves, the greatest prayer of man: that which asks not for victory, but for peace."

The Knotted Gun meanwhile has become a worldwide symbol. Replicas can be found at the Olympic Museum in Lausanne, at the waterfront of Cape Town, and at the Peace Park in Beijing. Ringo Starr designed a work of art capturing the same message to honor his late colleague. The rainbow-colored work of art stands in London. During a tour of the UN headquarters you can visit the peace treaty hall and the general gathering hall. Tours (with a guide) can be booked online.

Accessibility

Grand Central - 42nd Street

55

Barbetta Restaurant

321 WEST 46TH STREET, HELL'S KITCHEN

The magic of Italy in New York? Yes, it exists. It is within walking distance from Times Square. Those who visit the antique townhouse will experience a romantic décor of old Piedmont, where the owner and historian Laura Maioglio still owns a castle. The beautiful glass chandelier is originally from the collection of the royal house in Savoy. Barbetta is the oldest Italian restaurant in New York and is still owned by the same family as it was all those years ago. This high-class restaurant was the first to bring the espresso to New York, as well as famous Piedmont wines such as Barolo and Barbaresco. Many films and television episodes have been filmed here, including *The Departed* and *Sex and the City*.

The menu offers a lot of specialties. The fresh gnocchetti with delicious cheese sauce is one of the best. Meat and fish dishes are prepared by a team of excellent chefs, who work closely with Laura, who ensures the authentic Italian taste. Those who dine here in fall or winter should consider themselves lucky. This is the only restaurant in New York that uses truffle hounds in Northern Italy to sniff out the white truffles that are shaved over Barbetta's fresh pastas. If you're there during spring or summer, you can reserve a table in the romantic garden with its classic fountain. Afraid the "old" décor will soon change? Don't be, as Barbetta is the only restaurant in the United States of America that, in line with the Locali Storici d'Italia association, has been deemed a historical establishment. Barbetta will stay frozen in time forever. Laura married Dr. Günter Blobel, a medical Nobel Prize winner.

Accessibility

N **Q** **R**

49th Street

56

USS *Intrepid* Sea, Air & Space Museum

PIER 86, WEST 46TH STREET AND 12TH AVENUE, WEST MANHATTAN

Warships belong to superpowers.

Every generation of Americans has lived through one or even several wars. For many, a visit to the *Intrepid* is a patriotic honor. The ship survived the Second World War and five Japanese kamikaze attacks, though it did take on a bit of damage. You will see many veterans. Those who were decorated are honored in a separate gallery. There are four floors. A large number of military planes are on display. The Concorde and the Space Shuttle Enterprise, acquired in 2012, are also on display. Parents and children regularly visit the Exploration Hall where their motto is "hands on." Very popular is the flight simulator. You can also view the crew's narrow retreats. Children can climb all over. The Ready Room, where pilots receive their last instructions for missions behind the enemy line, might raise a few hairs on the back of one's neck. In 1966, Vietnam was the *Intrepid*'s target. The museum and flight deck were opened to the public in 1982.

Accessibility

A C E

50th Street

57

Berlin Wall

53RD STREET – 520 MADISON AVENUE, MIDTOWN EAST

n a wonderful spot between the skyscrapers is a part of the Berlin Wall. It is a piece that originally was part of the three-mile wall that was painted by Thierry Noir and Kiddy Citny in 1984. The graffiti artworks are statements that oppose the segregation of Berlin during the Cold War. The works are grim, but also ridicule the structure. After the fall of the wall, an auction house in Monaco sold part of the *Waldermarstrasse* in Kreuzberg to a New York businessman who placed them in front of his business. Now, staff sit on the benches against this strange background on their work breaks as passersby look at this scene. It has been a successful example of public street art. These are also the exact bits of wall that can be seen in the 1987 film *Der Himmel über Berlin* by Wim Wenders. The back side of the wall, the Eastern German side, is not painted. Such a ludicrous protest was not tolerated by the DDR authorities at the time.

The Berlin Wall

Artists: **Thierry Noir**
Kiddy Citny

These five original sections of the
rlin Wall marked the border between
East Berlin and West Berlin from
1961 - 1989

Accessibility

Fifth Avenue - 53rd Street

58

P. J. Clarke's Saloon

915 3RD AVENUE – EAST 55TH STREET, MIDTOWN EAST

Want to taste an excellent hamburger? Want to drink a beer or glass of wine amongst New Yorkers of all classes and ranks? Then you should visit the nineteenth-century bar that has stood against the test of time.

P. J. Clarke's is a historical icon amid the skyscrapers of New York. This bar and its menu have stayed authentic while the rest of the region changed from a workers' neighborhood to a yuppie neighborhood. This beautiful bar is visited often, and even by celebrities. It is a well-known fact that Frank Sinatra regularly ended up at P. J. Clarke's after a night on the town. Table twenty was his spot. Buddy Holly spontaneously, in this bar, asked his beloved to marry him. Johnny Mercer wrote his hit song "One for My Baby" on a napkin at the bar. At that same mahogany bar, Nat King Cole declared the cheeseburgers "the Cadillac of burgers." These burgers and the homemade fries make for a perfect dining experience. The same goes for the Caesar salad with a lot of anchovies, the juicy steak, and the rich New England clam chowder.

Recently the bar has been renovated. However, to the relief of many New Yorkers, the original atmosphere has remained. The jukebox still plays classics. Even the old broken telephone still has its place. If you lunch here on Saturday you might walk in the footsteps of Jackie Kennedy, who often brought her children, Caroline and John Jr., in on that day. Good food and drink, but the typical New York atmosphere makes a visit to "P. J." really remarkable.

Accessibility

E M

Lexington Avenue - 53rd Street

59

Franklin D. Roosevelt Four Freedoms Park

1 FDR FOUR FREEDOMS PARK, ROOSEVELT ISLAND

At the end of the sixties, the *New York Times* launched a campaign to name the Welfare Island in the Harlem River after the greatest twentieth-century president, and set up a monument accordingly. The newspaper called it the ideal place. The president could look out over the ocean that the Americans crossed to help Europe fight against the Nazis, and from the same spot he could look at the UN building. Governor Nelson Rockefeller and Mayor Lindsay announced the project in 1973, and called on architect Louis Kahn, who would later go on to create the Kimbell Art Museum in Texas, the Yale University Art Gallery, and the parliament building in Dhaka, Bangladesh. His style is representative of monumental and classic art. Kahn is a master of light and geometric shapes. He died in 1974, and soon after that, New York almost went bankrupt. It wasn't until March 29, 2010, that his project started.

It has since been finished. The monument is a collection of open spaces that lead the eye to one fixed point. There is a statue of Roosevelt, made by Jo Davidson in 1933. In this simple-version Greek-like temple without a roof, the four freedoms, as proclaimed by the president, are stated on the walls: freedom of speech, freedom of worship, freedom of want, and freedom of fear. For a unique way to travel to what was previously a sanatorium and prison island, take the tramway. It departs from the corner of 59th Street and 2nd Avenue. From the stop on the island it is a fifteen-minute walk south toward the park. There is also a bus and a subway. The view of Midtown is unique. Don't forget that it is closed on Tuesdays.

Accessibility

 Roosevelt Island

60

Bridges in Central Park

CENTRAL PARK

Men these days are often told that they are not romantic. If you wish to surprise your loved one, only do it if you are completely certain. Knowing if she will say yes to your proposal is always an uncertainty, as it is on the Heartbreak Bridge. This bridge, officially the Gapstow Bridge, got its nickname in 1898 when seamstress Helen Montclave wrote history by rejecting her partner Fredrick Huesen's proposal, immediately ending the relationship. This was not the last time a marriage proposal was rejected. However, the bridge also brings back warm memories. Everyone still remembers the scene of the film *Home Alone*. The protagonist Kevin bumps into the creepy pigeon lady. It wasn't long after that this lady was established to be very friendly and warm.

This historical place is easy on the eyes. The short bow between the green pond has a striking resemblance to the *Ponte di San Francesco* in San Remo along the Italian flower Riviera. Those who turn 360 degrees, probably out of love, will see the Plaza Hotel and the skyscrapers rising from the trees in the distance. During winter you will see ice-skaters at the Wollman Rink in the south. The brick bridge replaced the wooden bridge in 1896.

Another remarkable, romantic bridge in Central Park is the Bow Bridge. It is the second oldest bridge in America with a steel construction.

Accessibility

72nd Street - Central Park West

61

Musician, Composer, Educator, Arts Advocate, Humanitarian,
Visionary

Jazz at Lincoln Center
Salutes
Artistic Director
Wynton Marsalis

for his pivotal role in
founding Jazz at Lincoln Center and
the creation of Frederick P. Rose Hall, and on
25 years of creative contributions and leadership in
the rich and broad fields of jazz music.

Through his stunningly original composition,
commitment to education and swinging virtuosity,
he has indelibly enriched our music and
the American cultural landscape.

With love, admiration and deepest appreciation,
The Board of Directors, Artists and Staff of Jazz at Lincoln Center
November 14, 2005

Dizzy's Club Coca-Cola

10 COLUMBUS CIRCLE, UPPER WEST SIDE

New York is the jazz capital of the world and this club is considered "the Cadillac of jazz clubs." The club opened in 2004, and is settled on the fifth floor of the Time Warner Building. The ticket booth is in the building. Every guest at the bar or at a table has a breathtaking view of Columbus Circle and Central Park; it's a popular and romantic spot, especially at sunset. Remarkable cocktails such as "A Night in Tunisia" are served. The club swings in the spirit of its namesake, John Birks "Dizzy" Gillespie. The acoustics are especially good here. On Mondays, jazz students play, and on other nights you can hear some of the best bands from across the globe. Jazz legends such as Bill Charlap, Bobby Hutcherson, Cindy Blackman, Charles McPherson, and Dianne Reeves all played here. Even Stevie Wonder made a surprise appearance or two. For the first show at 7:30 p.m., the doors will open at 6 o'clock in the evening for those who wish to dine here. The cuisine is based on that of jazz cities such as Chicago, St. Louis, and New Orleans. Of course, you can order some Southern fried chicken here. This jazz club is a part of the jazz program at Lincoln Center. Every so often, a surprise act will play at the end of the night. We recommend booking a table early. Students receive a discount.

© Frank Steward for Jazz at Lincoln Center

Accessibility

59th Street - Columbus Circle

62

Rollerblades, Dancing, and Music in Central Park

CENTRAL PARK, 72ND STREET

New York swings best in Central Park. Fascinating, even breathtaking. Perhaps even join the Central Park Dance Skaters Association. You can enter the park from 72nd Street on the east side, as well as on the west side of the park. The skaters show off their best tricks. With some regularity, a skate truck appears and you can rent some roller skates for yourself. Around 3:00 p.m. on Saturdays and Sundays is when the spectacle really starts, and it runs from spring until autumn. Check www.cpdsa.org for the exact times and dates. If you visit the Lake at Central Park in the summer you will walk amongst a large group of people listening to David Ippolito. The guitarist started playing here in 1992 to earn enough money to buy some lunch. Since then he has become a Central Park phenomenon. He brings his own music, but also plays in other areas. Where and when? You can subscribe via www.thatguitarman.com to his mailing list. David promises to keep you updated.

Accessibility

72nd Street - Central Park West

63

Strawberry Fields

CENTRAL PARK WEST, 72ND STREET

John Lennon and Yoko Ono returned home from the studio on the night of December 8, 1980. At the entrance of the Dakota apartment complex, Mark Chapman shot four bullets into Lennon's back. Lennon could still run to the lobby and shout, "I'm shot." He fell to the ground while Yoko Ono supported his head. The doorman yelled to Chapman, "Do you know what you've done?" and called the emergency services. On the way to the hospital, Lennon lost 80 percent of his blood. Upon arrival at the hospital he was declared dead. In 1984, Mayor Koch opened the peace park Strawberry Fields (2.5 acres), across from Dakota in Central Park. Yoko Ono donated $1 million to the project. It was designed by Bruce Kelly. Since then, the park is known as a peace park in 121 countries. This tear-shaped oasis of plants, trees, and flowers introduces visitors from all over the world to the songs and peaceful memory of the "best Beatle." At its northern point are three water cypresses that often lose their needles. But, as a symbol of renewal, they regrow their needles every spring. The city of Naples donated an impressive mosaic of "Lennon's word": Imagine. Some of his ashes were spread across Strawberry Fields. Usually on weekends you will find many street performers giving their own rendition of many Beatles songs. Of course, they are most prominent on December 8 and October 9, the dates of his assassination and Lennon's birthday, respectively.

Accessibility

A **C** **B**

72nd Street - Central Park West

64

New York Historical Society Museum & Library

170 CENTRAL PARK WEST, UPPER WEST SIDE

The oldest museum of New York (1804) literally stands in the shadow of the famed Natural History Museum. Since its recent and radical renovation this museum holds even more surprises. It shows the history of America and the world from New York's perspective. The temporary display from past years, about slavery and AIDS, drew a lot of attention. The monumental museum displays a large variety of objects. There is a unique collection of the nineteenth-century Hudson River School that combined agricultural art with that of the Romantic era. The largest Tiffany glass collection in the world can be found here. The stained-glass windows displaying Henry Hudson's entry to America and the painting *Flags on Fifty-Seventh Street* by Frederick Childe Hassam are great pieces. Hassam is a celebrated American impressionist whose art, since the Kennedy years, has hung in the White House. President Obama has even placed one of his flag paintings in the Oval Office. Downstairs, there is a separate and interesting children's museum. Children become history detectives and learn in an interactive manner about New Yorkers from the past, such as the Dutch salesman's daughter Cornelia van Varick. The children's museum is aimed at ages eight to thirteen. You can end your visit in the stylish Café Storico, owned by Stephen Starr who made his name with the restaurant Buddakan. He was named "Restaurateur of the Year" by *Zagat* magazine. Italian dishes are served at Café Storico. If you'd rather try some American cuisine, we suggest visiting Isabella's at 359 Columbus Avenue, also aimed at families.

Accessibility

81st Street - Museum of Natural History

Fairway Market

**2127 BROADWAY/74TH STREET,
UPPER WEST SIDE**

For the best way to prepare for a picnic at Central Park, search no further. It first started as a fruit and vegetable stall in 1933, and since expanded across an entire covered block with its rightful slogan "Like No Other Market." During the seventies, Fairway discovered that Americans kept buying foreign produce but had no inclination as to where it originally came from. Thus, a bottle of olive oil with a beautiful label could be a great success, even if it came from an obscure factory. The owners of Fairway made their work into their hobby, their addiction, and toured for years on every street in the famous regions of Tuscany, Umbria, and Provence. Their fresh produce had to meet extremely high standards. Their employees soon became nutrition experts. Don't be surprised when someone explains to you with photo in hand from which tree which olive was picked. Since then, Fairway has roughly six hundred types of cheese, one hundred olive oils, and eighty types of coffee. Sushi, with all kinds of fish, warm meals—in short "everything" can be bought here. Fresh baguettes, cheesecake, donuts, and coleslaw (a botched word from the Dutch language) are also popular. There is also a giant section dedicated to organic products. On the second floor there is a restaurant where chef Mitchel London, who used to cook for former mayor Ed Koch, will prepare a fresh portion of macaroni and cheese and lots of other dishes for less than $15. Saturday and Sunday it can be very busy on Fairway's small pathways. This food mecca is popular throughout the nation due to the NBC television series *Farm to Fairway*. In other places in New York and its surroundings, Fairway has opened its stores, but Broadway will remain the flagship.

Accessibility

72nd Street

66

Salumeria Rosi
Parmacotto

283 AMSTERDAM AVENUE, UPPER WEST SIDE

An authentic piece of Italy in New York! In this store there is an assortment of the most delicious *salumi* sausages and cheeses from Tuscany and the surrounding districts of Parma. There is also an elaborate collection of Italian wines. What makes this delicacy paradise even more special are its indoor and outdoor dining areas on the street terrace. There is also a bar. Popular dishes include those with lots of smaller courses. Not just meat, but also cheese, pasta dishes, and salads. Ravioli, risotto, and lasagna are very popular even besides their famous pork dish. You can choose a special *assaggi* menu, which is made up of lots of finger-food dishes. The famed chef Cesare Casella is the dean of Italian Studies at the famous International Culinary Center. The interior is great with a special map of Italy, designed by Oscar winner Dante Ferretti. It is, of course, a great sign that many Italians visit this restaurant, which makes you feel like you've stepped right into an authentic piece of Italy.

Accessibility

1 2 3

72nd Street

67

Moooi

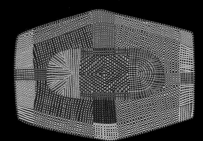

6 EAST 31ST STREET, NOMAD

oooi's Dutch design is conquering the United States in record time. Design director Marcel Wanders designed the interior of the Mondrian Hotel in Miami's trendy South Beach. He is also known for his artistic enclosures in the *New York Times* and the *Financial Times*. Some of his exhibitions are even in famous museums such as the MoMA and the Stedelijk Museum in Amsterdam. Since May 2015, Moooi has had a great showroom and store in Nomad, an up-and-coming neighborhood North of Madison Park and the Chrysler Building. Moooi's secret? Wanders tells us: "Moooi is a city design brand for the new world. We bring the coolest things together that collectively create an atmosphere of surprise and exceed expectations." Moooi fits the vibe of New York. The lamps, furniture, rugs, and photos are artwork in themselves, but the magic of Moooi is that it all fits together, nicely. Modern, classic, abstract, and figurative. One of its eye-catchers is a giant horse. Now that Moooi has established itself in New York, there is a certain expectation that the district North of Madison Park will quickly become a design hot spot, and will be a direct competitor of SoHo in South Manhattan.

moooi

Accessibility

6

33rd Street/Park Avenue

68

Carnegie Mansion
Cooper-Hewitt Design Museum

2 EAST 91ST STREET – FIFTH AVENUE, UPPER EAST SIDE

Carnegie, the richest man in the world, originally came from a poor Scottish family and worked his way up the market. He said: "The man who dies rich, dies disgraced." He decided to donate 90 percent of his fortune to building some four thousand libraries where people could develop their skills and come to understand that wars should be out of the question. This peace activist also donated toward the construction of what he called the "Temple of Peace," or in other words the Vredespaleis in The Hague. Initially he lived in New York on Millionaires' Row on 51st Street–Fifth Avenue. But the crude lifestyle of the rich and famous annoyed him. To the surprise of many, he bought a piece of land thirty blocks from there, in what then seemed to be part wilderness, and built a mansion with sixty-four rooms for his wife, daughter, and twenty staff members. Every morning, an organist would play favorite classic melodies so that the Carnegie family would wake up peacefully. The house was a great example of technological advancements, as it had an air-conditioning system and elevators. Carnegie delegated for a wine cellar to be built, and he had two full-grown trees from Connecticut placed in his humongous backyard. He loved Central Park and wandered along the Lake every day.

When he died in 1916, he left a large sum of money to his staff as well, as they were also like family to him. These days, the mansion is now part of the Cooper-Hewitt Design Museum that exhibits three thousand years of interior design and showcases many objects, from Parisian parasols to Tiffany's glass designs. Lincoln's steel chair is very popular among its American visitors. The museum once held the Beatles' Rolls-Royce. However, lots of things that Carnegie owned are no longer there, including the pipe organ.

Accessibility

 96th Street

69

The Ravine

101ST STREET, CENTRAL PARK WEST

s you enter Central Park via 101st Street, walk north, in the direction of the Pool, and start your trip through the Ravine at the Glen Span Arch. Go below the bowed bridge. Do you hear the soft rumble of a streaming creek? The flowing waterfalls? The complete peace of this rich, bushy area? You wouldn't expect to see this in New York's concrete jungle, but here it is. Many New Yorkers who have lived in the city for years have never explored this northwesterly part of Central Park. Its architect, Frederick Law Olmsted, was inspired by the beautiful landscapes painted by the Hudson River School. Even outside of the City there are breathtaking parts of nature, from the Hudson River Valley to the Catskill Mountains. Even farther north are the Adirondack Mountains. Amid the growing metropolis, Olmsted constructed his own romantic landscape based on these rocks in nature. In the Ravine, nature is the boss. With exception to the footpath, fallen trees are not removed. Hundreds of flowers and herbs such as aster and goldenrods can be found here. There are dozens of bird species, some quite unusual for a city area. At the Loch, a fast-streaming creek, a bittern, related to the heron, was spotted. The most beautiful rocky bridge, the Huddlestone Arch, can be found. It was built in 1866 and is supported by its own weight and gravity. The Ravine and the Loch are also part of the North Woods. At the end of the Loch you will find the Lasker Rink and Pool. In winter this is an ice-skating rink; in summer it is a public pool.

Accessibility

103rd Street

70

El Museo del Barrio

1230 FIFTH AVENUE – 104TH STREET, EAST HARLEM

This colorful and quaint museum was created out of a civil movement in the sixties; attention was sought after for the culture of the immigrant children from Puerto Rico and other Spanish-speaking countries. In East Harlem, where most of its inhabitants were from a Latino background, educational courses were successfully set up and directed with everybody's culture in mind. It's not too far-fetched to realize that this museum was originally set up to be a classroom. After lots of moving around, a large collection of pre-Columbian art and modern art can be admired here. There is a large collection of Taíno art. These Taíno folk lived, at the time of Columbus's discovery of America, in the Caribbean. Many Taíno women were raped by Spaniards and taken to their new homes. Eventually, the original population died from some of the diseases that the Spaniards brought with them. Art and social history overlap each other here. The museum is now established in the neoclassical Heckscher Building close to the outtermost point of Central Park. There is a fine restaurant that serves ethnic dishes. Their gift shop is well worth a visit. On Saturdays, the museum organizes an interesting walk through Spanish Harlem. The surrounding areas with all sorts of murals breathe the atmosphere of the museum.

Accessibility

 103rd Street

71

Sylvia's Restaurant

324 LENOX AVENUE (MALCOLM X BOULEVARD), BETWEEN 126TH AND 127TH STREETS, CENTRAL HARLEM

Nicknamed the "Queen of Soul Food" is a fifty-year-old restaurant called Sylvia's, in Central Harlem. Sylvia Wood, whose family still runs the restaurant, took her "Southern cooking" talents to an area that was very popular in the twenties because of music legends such as Duke Ellington. As other places in the United States were taking on welfare, Harlem remained poverty stricken. In the eighties there was a crack epidemic, and criminal activity was on the rise. However, Sylvia's remained a safe haven. Even during the great street riots in 1964, the restaurant remained just out of shot, although a few windows may have been ruined. The poor black inhabitants of the area felt at home in this simple living-room restaurant where food was served "with love." Harlem has the greatest density of Baptist churches in the United States. On Sundays there is still a famous gospel brunch and on Saturdays is the jazz brunch. Popular dishes such as chicken and waffles, barbecue ribs, and macaroni and cheese are still served here. As a concession to the current health culture they also serve grilled meat. The middle class has been reestablished in Harlem in line with Bill Clinton's office and the success of the social education project Harlem Children's Zone. With the second Harlem Renaissance, property prices skyrocketed. Sylvia's clientele has changed, though the restaurant has still kept its essence and atmosphere. Those who visit this restaurant stand in the steps of Nelson Mandela, Muhammad Ali, and Oprah Winfrey. And, of course, Barack Obama. Sylvia Wood's famous cookbooks have been sold here since her death in 2012, at the age of eighty-six.

Accessibility

2 **3** 125th Street

72

Abyssinian Baptist Church

132 WEST 138TH, BETWEEN ADAM CLAYTON POWELL JR. BOULEVARD AND LENOX AVENUE, CENTRAL HARLEM

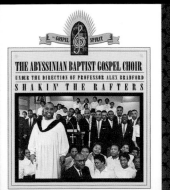

Harlem has the greatest density of Baptist churches in the United States. The Abyssinian draws the most attention amid its four hundred Baptist counterparts. The name refers to the Ethiopian or Abyssinian "free" immigrants. Under Reverend Clayton Powell Sr.'s leadership, the church community moved in the twenties. This was during the time of the Harlem Renaissance. From the South, many African Americans established themselves in Harlem, where blues and jazz were all the rage. The impressive church was first used in 1923. Its architecture is neo-Gothic and neo-Tudor with a large number of ornaments on the buttresses. The church, under Powell's leadership, grew to become one of the largest Protestant church communities in the United States. A German man named Dietrich Bonhoeffer "interned" at the church in 1931. He was very interested in the principles and methods of the black church elders in their fight for social justice. He became a great protestor of Hitler's work back in Germany. Clayton Powell Jr. followed in his father's footsteps and became a reverend in 1938. As a national civil rights leader, he organized, together with Reverend Martin Luther King Jr., the march in Washington. This was the same occasion on which Martin Luther King Jr. gave his "I Have a Dream" speech. Every Sunday there are two services, at 9:00 a.m. and 11:00 a.m., which you are welcome to sit in on as long as you are dressed in your Sunday best. It is a unique experience to hear the well-known choir sing the roof off the place. Alternatively, there is also an evening service at 7:00 p.m. You can book a "Harlem Gospel Tour" at www.harlemspirituals.com.

Accessibility

2 **3**   135th Street

73

Morris-Jumel Mansion

65 JUMEL TERRACE, 160TH STREET, WASHINGTON HEIGHTS

The oldest house in Manhattan (1765) still stands in Washington Heights. This monument and museum offer an amazing view of the Harlem River, the Bronx, the Hudson River, and even Long Island. At the start of the American Revolution, the British owner Roger Morris moved to England. Between September 14 and October 20, 1776, General George Washington used this mansion as his temporary headquarters during the American Revolutionary War. President George Washington later dined here with future presidents Thomas Jefferson and John Adams on July 10, 1790. From 1810 the mansion fell into the hands of rich wine tradesman Stephen Jumel. His eccentric wife Eliza led an adventurous life during the times of moneyed aristocracy. In Paris she bought many antiques to refine the mansion. She claimed also to have bought a bed and two chairs from Napoleon. When her husband found out that prior to their marriage she had worked as a prostitute, their marriage began to suffer. Stephen died from falling onto a pitchfork. It was rumored that Eliza let him bleed to death. The widow then married Aaron Burr, the controversial previous vice president. He killed his political competitor Alexander Hamilton in a duel. In 1836, on the day their divorce had become official, he died. Eliza stayed behind, suffering from dementia, and remained in the mansion. She was so attached to the house that her spirit is mentioned in many of its ghost stories. Up until now her spirit has only been seen in the dark. The architecture of the house is in an impressive Palladio style. The rooms of the museum provide an interesting display of life in the nineteenth century. Closed on Mondays and Tuesdays.

Accessibility

163rd Street - Amsterdam Avenue

The Cloisters

99 MARGARET CORBIN DRIVE, FORT TYRON PARK,
NORTH MANHATTAN

f you're looking to escape the modern, busy city of New York for a few hours, visiting the Cloisters would be an excellent choice. This is thanks to the filthy-rich Good Samaritan who made the construction of this building possible during the thirties. He bought a large collection of medieval sculptures from the well-known American sculptor George Grey Barnard for the museum. He also had the ground relaid in Fort Tyron Park to build the museum on top of it. To protect the unique view of the Hudson River, he also bought the greenery on the other side of the river in the state of New Jersey. He donated works of art from his own collection, including one of the most famous pieces, *The Unicorn Tapestries*. This mysterious, mighty unicorn from legends is said to have performed many miracles such as transforming poisoned water into a health elixir. Only a virgin could control the animal, which often lead to erotic consequences. With regard to its mysterious properties, it's easy to understand why scenes from Harry Potter were filmed here.

It's remarkable to note that the Cloisters are actually made up of several overlapping European cloisters. Together they form a unique ensemble with all sorts of passageways. You will see Roman as well as early and late Gothic styles. Not to mention the large number of paintings, stained-glass windows, and religious artifacts. Many of the gardens represent real medieval herb gardens. The architect was Charles Collens, a co-designer of the Riverside Church elsewhere in New York City. The Cloisters are part of the Metropolitan Museum. As you make an exit to the subway, you will stumble across the New Leaf Restaurant in the park, owned by Bette Midler, also known for her environmental awareness.

Accessibility

 Dyckman Street

SHORAKKOPOCH

ACCORDING TO LEGEND, ON THIS SITE OF THE
PRINCIPAL MANHATTAN INDIAN VILLAGE, PETER MINUIT
IN 1626, PURCHASED MANHATTAN ISLAND, FOR TRINKETS
AND BEADS THEN WORTH ABOUT 60 GUILDERS.

THIS BOULDER ALSO MARKS THE SPOT WHERE
A TULIP TREE (LIRIODENDRON TULIPIFERA) GREW TO A HEIGHT
OF 165 FEET AND A GIRTH OF 20 FEET. IT WAS, UNTIL
ITS DEATH IN 1933 AT THE AGE OF 280 YEARS, THE
LAST LIVING LINK WITH THE RECKGAWAWANG INDIANS
WHO LIVED HERE.

DEDICATED AS PART OF
NEW YORK CITY'S 300TH ANNIVERSARY CELEBRATION
BY THE PETER MINUIT POST 1247, AMERICAN LEGION
JANUARY 1954

Peter Minuit's Plaque

215TH STREET – INDIAN ROAD, INWOOD HILL PARK, NORTH MANHATTAN

And so, we have reached the last destination. The hardest. We are standing at the edge of a gigantic primeval forest. This part of Manhattan has been left untouched. There are hills and dense bushland. In multiple places you will find boulders. Behind one of these boulders is a plaque that describes how Peter Minuit bought Manhattan from the Native Americans. Archives suggest we follow Indian Road toward the Indian caves. On the right you will pass a pond. But where is it? We search every nook and cranny. If we walk into the woods we will get lost. But we're in luck; an old lady sits on the bench across from where we're standing. We talk to her and instantly this friendly, local historian, Mary van Hoorn, explains where we need to be. "It's southwest, just keep following the path." And, indeed, there it is. Behind a large boulder we discover the plaque that was placed here in 1954. The text tells us that in 1938 the largest tree of Manhattan stood here, a magnolia tree. It got blown over in the storm, but where it stood is where the transaction took place. Researchers at the New Netherlands Institute note that according to legend, the transaction actually took place in Battery Park. Mary tells us the neighborhood still believes in the story. However it happened, it remains an intriguing tale! Mary points to the highest railway bridge: "When it becomes dark, the coyotes run across the bushed hills and run into the forest. This place is swarming with animals." A wilderness oasis, in Manhattan!

Accessibility

 Dyckman Street